User Experience Innovation

Christian Kraft

D1523102

Apress·

User Experience Innovation

ISBN-13 (pbk): 978-1-4302-4149-2

ISBN-13 (electronic): 978-1-4302-4150-8

Distributed to the book trade worldwide by Springer-Verlag New York, Inc., 233 Spring Street, 6th Floor, New York, NY 10013. Phone 1-800-SPRINGER, fax 201-348-4505, e-mail orders-ny@springer-sbm.com, or visit http://www.springeronline.com.

For information on translations, please contact us by e-mail at info@apress.com, or visit http://www.apress.com.

Apress and friends of ED books may be purchased in bulk for academic, corporate, or promotional use. eBook versions and licenses are also available for most titles. For more information, reference our Special Bulk Sales–eBook Licensing web page at http://www.apress.com/info/bulksales.

Contents

About the Author

Christian Kraft was born in Denmark in 1967. After graduating his Masters of Electronic Engineering in 1991 at the University of Aalborg, he joined the mobile phone industry when some of the first digital handheld mobile phones were being developed. Christian has today worked in the Mobile Device industry for more than 18 years, 14 years for Nokia, and 4 years for Sony and Hagenuk. Most of the years have been spent with strong focus on user interaction design, user experience design, and innovation.

Christian is sole- or co-inventor of some of the most used User Interfaces in the world from Nokia, as well as a number of big- and small-user experience innovations which have been and still are used by millions of mobile device users. With more than 100 patents filed under his name including a number of highly successful innovations for Nokia, Christian has proven his ability to create successful user experience innovation; he may well be one of the top three inventors in the Mobile Device industry.

You may visit his home page on kraftux.com.

What Other People Say

Harri Kiljander, PhD, Director User Experience Design, F-Secure Corporation:

"If you are working in a fast-paced new product development project or have just been given the task of figuring out why an earlier product or software release is not a raving success among its targeted user base, this book is for you. Written by a creative and productive user experience designer with a long and successful track record in user experience innovation, this is a practical cookbook for product developers, marketeers, strategists, and user experience practitioners alike.

I learned to know Christian in the late 1990s when we were exploring future mobile phone user interaction opportunities in the corporate research unit of Nokia. That concept design work later found its way to about 1.5 billion Nokia mobile phones running the S40 software platform and user interface. Later on, we collaborated around topics like text input research and the seminal Navi-key user interface design.

During his career, Christian has produced and contributed to numerous innovations and patents in the field of human-computer interaction, and in this book he unfolds his experiences and insights of the user experience what and how, describing recipes to be followed and warning about dead ends to be avoided. Equipped with the user experience toolbox introduced in this book, you will get a head start in creating the next product your users and customers will fall in love with."

Michael McKay, Sr Director, Design Language and Mobile Experiences, Yahoo!Design:

"Creating breakthrough innovations is something most companies dream of and pursue. Few have succeeded and many talks and books have been made about the subject. Christian Kraft is one of those authentic innovators who actually has been there and created winning concepts. He is behind 100's of patentable concepts that millions of people have used. I had the pleasure of working with Christian while at Nokia, where we joined his unique ideation techniques with User Driven Innovation into a cross organizational ideation hub.

In this book, Christian invites us into his special universe of User Experience Innovation. Christian shares stories from the birth of the telecom era with us. We are presented with the background of the first game launched in a mobile phone device and several other now iconic features. He shows how the universal values of curiosity, creativity and persistence can drive innovation into the future."

Panu Korhonen, Managing Director, Nordkapp:

"Christian is the most productive inventor that I've ever seen. If you need to get convinced, just check out how many times his name can be found in the patent databases.

Innovation requires creativity, persistence, attention to detail, and a very pragmatic mindset. Christian has all of this. I'm happy that he is sharing his secrets behind his innovation power in this practical and helpful book. It's a must read if you want to be a better innovator."

Erik Anderson, Vice President, Strategy, Business Development, and Portfolio Management, Nokia:

"I have worked with Christian over many years at Nokia. Christian is a classic "ideas man," one of the most creative at Nokia, with many innovations and patents to his name."

Peter Dam Nielsen, Customer Experience Leader, Schneider Electric:

"I have had the pleasure to work closely with Christian Kraft during almost a decade in Nokia Mobile Phones. During this time, Christian Kraft has been a constant source of inspiration to me and enriched my professional innovation abilities to a degree that made me a key inventor in Nokia and made me dedicate my professional life to constantly seek better and newer ways of meeting and exceeding the customer's expectations.

With this book, Christian Kraft has deservedly established himself as one of the pioneers within User Experience Innovation and I am convinced that with this book, not only larger corporations who seek methods to increase creativity and put more focus on innovation, but also individuals who want to make innovation more tangible and concretize their ideas into intellectual property rights, will have an extremely valuable tool".

Acknowledgements

I would like to thank my numerous colleagues, especially at Nokia: those who gave me freedom to pursue my ideas, those who appreciated my ideas, those who initiated or inspired great ideas, those who helped or showed me new ways of innovating and those who have supported my ideas.

Special thanks go to Peter Dam Nielsen, who has been my sparring partner in User Experience Innovation for more than ten years and with whom I have co-created a large number of successful user experience innovations as well as methods for creating successful innovations. I guess that around half of my patents are due to my long sparring with him.

I also want to give a big thank to my girlfriend for being very patient while writing this book.

Finally, thanks to Søren Engelbrecht, imagepro.dk for the photo of me.

Introduction

Many companies have found themselves in the situation of bringing a great product, service, or feature to the market, only to discover that the consumers simply didn't get it. Other companies have brought to the market products that became successful without the companies having any clue why.

Some may conclude that innovation is hence about pure luck. Nothing could be more wrong. Others may argue that perceived innovation can only come from companies that consumers already perceive as being highly innovative. My simple counter-question is, How did these companies build up a brand as being innovative in the first place?

Very often, the success of products, services, webpages, and even companies and brands comes back to one single thing: *successful user experience innovation.*

The Importance of User Experience

User experience is basically the sum or *flow* of feelings that the customer gets when using your device, webpage, or system. In many businesses, the user experience of the product is already the key battlefield. Forget about launching the newest technologies unless you have designed a great user experience around them. Being first is no longer enough, and the winner is often the company that makes the new thing better than anyone else has.

Just look at the mobile phone industry. Was Apple the first company to apply touch screens to a smart phone? No. Touch screens existed in the mobile phone industry at least ten years before Apple launched the first iPhone. But Apple managed to create an excellent user experience for this old technology. Nokia, which used to be seen as the leader in user experience, failed for several years to create even an acceptable user experience for touch screen devices, and this is now reflected very much in the market situation and in which companies run off with the profits.

I will not claim that the methods described in this book are perfect, but I can say that these methods have helped me personally to create more than 100 filed patents, and they have helped me to create a number of truly successful user experience innovations for Nokia when Nokia was still seen as one of the top ten most innovative companies in the world. And when I say *successful user experience,* for me that means that I have seen or heard of a large number of users that actually loved my contributions to the mobile phone industry. My professional happiness does not depend on what my managers or the CEO says, but what I hear from real users.

The Goal for This Book

My goal in this book is to share my methods for innovating so that you can try them out and put them into practice for yourself. They will help you create truly successful user experience innovations, which may not only help your company or organization to become profitable, but also help you grow as a user experience expert or innovator.

Creating successful user experience innovation for your product will not only make your product more successful, but it can actually change the rules of an entire industry. I have personally had the luck to suggest user experience innovations that not only changed me and the company I worked for, but also the entire industry. For example, I managed to create the first SMS chat feature, as well as the first-ever game for a mobile device. And the customers loved these simple features since they covered real user needs.

Motivation

My view is that user experience already is—or soon will be—the key battleground for all types of consumer products, spanning from PC software to webpages to devices, from social websites to remote controls, from word-processing software to portable music players, from smart phones to low-end phone devices, and more. If you in the consumer business market fail to meet rising requirements from the end user, then you and your company may soon become obsolete. That is a fact.

User experience and user experience *innovation* are becoming the key competitive factors in more and more industries. Consumers are demanding products that are not only easy to use but also joyful and fun to use. Consumers will choose the products that put a smile on their face when using the product. In other words, consumers will choose products with a great user experience.

Why This Book?

You may find hundreds of books describing how to create good usability, how to listen to customers, and how to create consumer insight. And you may even find a lot of literature describing how to involve users in your design process. But you will find very few books giving very concrete methods on how to create ideas and innovations around user experiences.

To fill the gap in the literature, I will in this book describe tangible and straightforward methods on how you can create potentially successful user experience innovation. The methods and approaches are all based on methods that I have created, used, or applied successfully during my 18 years of creating user experience innovations for the mobile device industry, most of those years with Nokia. And even though the methods may seem simple, I can assure you that they work.

This book starts by giving guidance on how to achieve the basic foundation for all successful user experience innovation—namely how to identify target users, how to identify user needs, and how to find core tasks that the user performs when using your product.

Based on these three core elements—target users, their needs, and core tasks—I describe how to easily create successful user experience innovation in 17 different ways, spanning from how to directly use core tasks to create user experience innovation to how to create positive surprises and playful user experiences for the end user.

User experience innovation is an approach that can be applied to any business—from situations such as purchasing tickets at a train station, to the experience users get when entering physical shops, to the experience when operating a specific device, webpage, or system.

However, in this book I focus primarily on methods that can be used to create and design true and successful innovations for devices, webpages, and systems—which in this book will be called *products*. And I will mainly focus on products that are designed for consumer-focused markets.

My hope is that you will find one or ideally several of my methods and approaches useful and applicable for your specific design task, and I will look forward to seeing more great user experience innovations out there.

Overview of Successful User Experience Innovation Methods

There are hundreds or maybe thousands of well-documented methods on how to create new ideas. Many classical methods of creating ideas, however, have one important flaw: they do not take into account what the users need, what they like, what their passions are, what they have difficulties with, and so forth. And hence the ideas that come out may not likely be relevant for the end users.

Successful user experience innovation always starts with the consumer in focus. The methods I suggest in this book approach user experience innovations from different angles, but they all keep the main focus on consumers and their needs.

Overview of Methods and Chapters

This book contains two short introductory chapters followed by 17 chapters giving tangible methods for user experience innovation. Following is a quick summary of the content:

- *Chapter 1: User Experience and Why It Matters*: Introduces you to what user experience is, including some basic terms related to user experience.

- *Chapter 2: Innovating in User Experience*: When is a user experience innovation a success? How did Apple manage to change the rules of the smart phone industry with a single product? What is important for your company or product to become successful? These and other questions are answered in this chapter.

- *Chapter 3: Identifying Target Users*: Discusses identifying and defining who you are targeting, which is absolutely key for creating successful user experience innovation. This chapter will give you some methods on how to identify your target users.

- *Chapter 4: Identifying User Needs*: Gives guidance on how to find the user needs of your target users. User needs are the basis of all user experience innovation.

- *Chapter 5: Identifying Core Tasks*: Provides methods for identifying current and future core tasks for your product. Core tasks can be used directly or indirectly for user experience innovation.

- *Chapter 6: Innovating Around Core Tasks*: Describes how to come up with user experience innovations directly based on the core tasks that users perform using your product.

- *Chapter 7: Innovating for New Technologies*: Describes a tangible method for creating user experience innovation around technologies by examining basic user needs.

- *Chapter 8: Innovating for Applications*: Describes methods to create user experience innovation by focusing on how applications can be linked together seamlessly.

- *Chapter 9: Relieving the Pain*: Shows how you can identify pain points in the user experience of your existing product(s). I will also describe how removing pain points from your user experience can improve your overall user experience radically. Finally, you will realize how you can use your pain points to create successful user experience innovations.

- *Chapter 10: Innovating Around First Impressions*: Suggests methods to improve and innovate around the first impressions of your webpage, device, or system. The first impression is essential for your product and how it is received and perceived in the market.

- *Chapter 11: Creating Positive Surprises: The Wow Factor*: Covers the importance of creating a wow factor for your product. Creating small—or big—positive surprises can change your product from a mediocre product to a winning product. Positive surprises and wow are key factors in successful user experience innovation.

- *Chapter 12: Innovating Around an Ecosystem*: Helps you think beyond your product to the wider experience in which the product is used. User experience innovation is not only about improving the core of your product, but also very much about innovating for the entire ecosystem of your product.

- *Chapter 13: Innovating with Lead Users*: Why bother creating innovation inside the company if you can have lead users help you in the innovative process? This chapter describes tangible methods for this.

- *Chapter 14: Copying with Pride*: Talks about copying and building upon the innovations of others. Most successful innovations in the world were not new when they were launched, but rather became successful because an innovating company came up with just the right implementation, or because the company applied an existing innovation to a new type of product or platform. This chapter will describe how you can copy with pride—but at the same time making sure to do it right.

- *Chapter 15: Innovating Around Paradoxes*: Teaches how to resolve and benefit from conflicting needs. Paradoxes include conflicting user needs and conflicting needs from your shareholders and your management. In resolving paradoxes, you will find great opportunity to create successful products.

- *Chapter 16: Innovating Around Context Awareness*: Suggests tangible methods to innovate around situational awareness in your products. Context awareness is the ability for your product to know the situation that your user is in, where the user is, and what he or she may want to do. Context awareness can be a goldmine of potential successful innovation.

- *Chapter 17: Innovating Around New Products and Users*: Walks you through using all previously described methods to create a superb user experience for a product with a new target user group, or for a completely new product.

- *Chapter 18: Prototyping and Verifying Solutions*: Goes through tangible and simple methods to create prototypes and verify solutions with target users. Your user experience innovation ideas need to be verified with your target users, ideally at every step of your iterative innovation process. For any verification you will need one or more prototypes of some sort.

- *Chapter 19: Meeting Organizational Challenges*: Describes approaches to use in challenging attitudes and old ways of thinking that get in the way of bringing successful user experience design to an organization or product. User experience innovations and ideas will never be heard in a majority of organizations and companies. This is very sad, not only for you as a user experience person, but also for your company. Tomorrow's battleground for most consumer products will be on the user experience front, and if your company does not catch up, then the reality of losing market share and profits will be inevitable. This chapter can help you sell the need for good user experience design to management and colleagues.

- *Conclusion*: Provides a short wrap-up to the book.

Figure I shows the methods described in this book in conjunction with inputs such as user needs and technology choices. Looking at the figure you can begin to get a feel for how you can start thinking of user experience fro the standpoint of user needs and use the methods in this book to work through to successful product solutions.

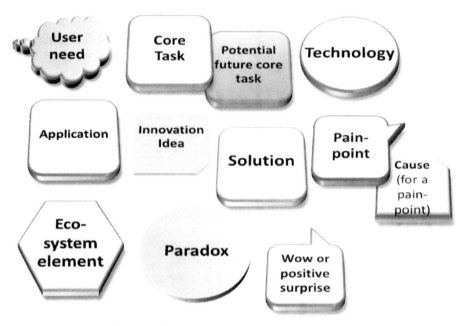

Figure 1. *Overview of the methods for successful user experience innovation described in this book*

You will realize that several of the methods I describe in the following chapters are pretty obvious and straightforward. That is OK. Making these straightforward is the entire goal of the book. Demystifying user experience innovation and making it applicable to any company, organization, or person is precisely my purpose.

I am not claiming that the methods in this book are the only right ways to create true user experience innovations. But I am claiming that they have worked for me. I have personally used all the described methods, and very often with success. The methods have led me to success when it comes to creating user experience innovations that consumers love, and that are profitable and patentable.

User Experience and Why It Matters

1

This chapter will give a brief introduction to and definitions of terms like *user experience, creativity, innovation*, and *successful user experience innovation*.

Many books have been written to define user experience, to define innovation, to boost creativity, and so forth, but the scope of this book is not to dwell on definitions and academic descriptions of these terms. Many other authors have already done this much better.

So this introductory chapter is rather here to just lay the ground for the tangible and intangible methods and approaches for user experience innovation that I will outline in the remainder of the book.

What Is User Experience?

According to ISO standards, *user experience* is defined as "a person's perceptions and responses that result from the use or anticipated use of a product, system or service."[1]

However, I will twist this basically correct definition a little. I would describe user experience as the *feelings* that the user gets when using a product. Using feelings as a comparison model allows us to understand that the user experience can be anything from hate to love. From anger to happiness. From indifference to passion. From expectance to nostalgia. From pride to humiliation. And so forth.

User Experience Curve

When using a product (or when purchasing a device, sending it for repair, etc.), you can try to imagine the feelings that the user will have in different situations. Positive feelings mean that the user experience curve goes up, Negative feelings mean that the curve goes down. If the curve goes down too much—or drops repeatedly during the process—you will most likely lose the customer even before purchasing; or the

---

[1] ISO FDIS 9241-210:2009, Ergonomics of human system interaction - Part 210: Human-centered design for interactive systems (formerly known as 13407), International Organization for Standardization (ISO), Switzerland.

customer may end up being pretty unhappy most of the time using your product. And they will most likely not purchase a product from you again.

Figure 1-1 shows an example of this "user experience curve" in a first-usage situation for a mobile device.

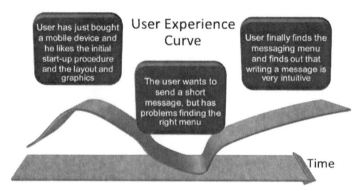

Figure 1-1. Example of user experience curve

One problem with feelings (and hence the user experience) is that different people react differently in different situations. And the same person may get different feelings in the same situation depending on the context. If the user, for example, had a very stressful day, he may easily drop rapidly on the user experience curve compared to the same user going shopping on a relaxing summer vacation.

And as with a personal relationship, the feelings may change over time, or even from day to day. Certain things may even make us go from happiness to anger in just seconds (e.g., if a software program crashes when you have just been using it for an hour, typing a long letter). Other things may become annoying to use when the user knows that there are better solutions out there.

The goal is of course to maximize the positive moments for users when they're using your product. And ideally to make your consumers love your product—at least some or most of the time.

Another very important element—which is also described further in Chapter 9—is to eliminate the worst negative feelings during usage of a product. One negative user experience may need ten good experiences to make the user happy again.

Expectations and User Experience

User experience is very much about expectations. Generally, if customers have low initial expectations, then your product can more easily surprise the customers positively (Figure 1-2).

Time

Figure 1-2. Ideal user experience curve with low initial end-user expectations

But for superb products and sustainable brands, you actually *want* the customers to have high expectations. High expectations basically mean that you can charge more for your products. If you manage to build up high user expectations for your products, however, then you need to match (or ideally, exceed) these expectations for your next product. Not fulfilling the expectations may be fatal (see Figure 1-3).

Time

Figure 1-3. User experience curve when not fulfilling high initial end-user expectations

Expectations may depend on cultural differences, how customers perceive your brand, and a number of other things. But the essential part in the context of this book is to realize how a good—or bad—user experience will affect the expectations of your product.

For a small local grocery shop, the customers may not expect the shop to have a full-blown superbly designed web page with photos and prices of all items, online sales, and so on.

End-user expectations of the web page for a grocery shop may initially be low partly because the customers do not expect that from a small shop, but also partly because most users may not have a *need* for a high-end web page for such a shop. Many grocery buyers often prefer to enter the physical shop where they can touch, feel, and immediately purchase the products.

However, these low end-user expectations can also be seen as a potential opportunity for a grocery shop that wants to stand out. If the owners actually choose to design a cool-looking web page with great user experience and online shopping, this may just be the thing that leads some customers into their shop and not the one next door.

A good user experience can hence easily and quickly *change* customers' expectations. Expectations for your product are hence not fixed. They will in fact change every time you—or your competition—raises the bar by providing successful user experience innovations.

Anecdote

Some years ago, most people did not *feel a need* to own a smart phone, since smart phones were seen as complicated high-end devices designed and intended for business people (and they *were* in fact complicated to use).

End users may have had a latent need for many of the core tasks that a smart phone could perform, but the hassle to get these tasks fulfilled was simply too overwhelming.

The first iPhone (Figure 1-4) changed the perception of a smart phone being complicated to use. And Apple changed the expectations of millions of users by allowing them to solve desired core tasks in an elegant and easy way.

Figure 1-4. Apple changed the perception and expectations of smart phones.

When Apple launches a new product, the expectations are always very high from their customers. And Apple can only survive by fulfilling or exceeding the customers' expectations.

User Experience vs. Consumer Experience

User experience is limited to the actual usage of your product. Consumer experience, on the other hand, also covers the experiences that the user gets when looking up your product on the Internet, when seeing TV commercials, when entering a shop, when giving the product back for repair, when replacing the product with another, and so forth.

In this book, I will focus mainly on the user experience; however, many of the methods described in this book will also apply to the consumer experience. Some of these methods will even directly touch upon how to innovate around the consumer experience (e.g., when I start describing methods to innovate the user experience around the ecosystem in Chapter 12).

First Impressions Last

Whether we like to admit it or not, we judge people very much on the first impression we get of them. Glance at the person in Figure 1-5. Do you have an impression? Very likely you do have an impression, and it's from just one quick glance at a single image.

Figure 1-5. First impressions last.

There is also first impression for the user experience of a product. If your product needs eight hours charging before you can turn it on, if the user is faced with tens of difficult questions before you can start using your web page, or if the user's impression of the sales shop she enters is far from optimal, then you have given the user a very bad first impression of your product.

In the best case, the result is that the customers will lower their expectations respectively. This is, however, not good for any business, since it will also lower the price expectations of your product.

In the worst case, you will lose existing customers, or you will leave the customers with a first impression that can take at least ten great user experiences to change into a positive overall experience. Figure 1-6 shows an example of how a poor first impression might take some time to overcome.

Time

Figure 1-6. Example of user experience curve when the first impression of your product is bad

Many web page developers in the world do not understand that a Flash introduction means losing a large amount of customers (even if it looks cool), simply because it may take tens of seconds or even minutes to load. Many owners of social websites mistakenly believe that users want to tell everything about themselves, and spend several minutes doing this even before they know what to use the website for. Many device manufacturers ask users to configure complex settings before even letting them get into the core functions of the device.

So, in other words, your first impression lasts a lot longer than you think—and a bad first impression may already mean that you have lost a large amount of customers.

For tangible methods on how to create successful user experience innovation around first impressions, refer to the approach described in Chapter 10.

Long-Term User Experience

Many devices, web pages, software packages, and so on focus solely on the first impression. This may in some cases make your consumers choose your product, but the same consumers will only return to your product next time if they also feel good during daily use of your product.

Again, long-term user experience resembles a personal relationship. Yes, the first impression may make you get interested in or engaged with a person, but you will not maintain a relationship with the person unless they give you something back in the longer term.

Long-term user experience is hence just as important as the first impression—at least if you want your customers to come back to you next time. Ideally, you want a user experience curve similar to that in Figure 1-7, showing more or less constant growth in satisfaction over time. There will always be a few dips in the road, but the overall trend should be upward.

Long
Time

Figure 1-7. Ideal user experience curve for long-term usage

A good long-term user experience is characterized by a daily joy when using a product. It is characterized by evolving together with the user, and by a growing "love" of your product from your users.

The result of a good long-term user experience is that the end user will want to return to your product again and again. Usually a good long-term user experience is achieved by tiny things that keep surprising the user—or just making the user feel that he is in control of the product. Continuous successful improvements and upgrades of your product are also important for the long-term user experience.

Positive Surprises (Wows)

A key element of a good user experience is providing small surprises for the user. These can also be called *wows*. These surprises of course need to be positive, and they can make people think or even say the word *wow*. Figure 1-8 shows an advertisement with a certain wow effect.

A wow could be something like a great and logical graphical layout where the user thinks, "Wow, this looks good." It could also be a user interaction that is designed in a playful way. Playfulness is a very essential part of wows and positive surprises.

Figure 1-8. Example of wow. Credits and description: Giant constrictor snake squeezing complete Copenhagen citybus. Advertising Agency: Bates Y&R, Copenhagen, Denmark. Creative Director: Ib Borup. Art Director: Peder Schack. Agency Producers: Josephine Winther-Poupinel, Steen Nøhr. Other credit: Erich Karsholt. The Print Ad titled Snake Bus was done by Bates Y&R advertising agency for brand: Copenhagen Zoo in Denmark. It was released in Dec 2009.

Wows and positive surprises can also happen when the user discovers a small, intelligent function that, for example, helps him type text faster. Or they can refer to the pleasure the user feels when he finds a shortcut for an often used function on a web page.

Positive surprises are needed on every level of interaction and usage, but focus should be made on core tasks that the user performs. Designing great interaction elements that users do not need or may not find is a waste of resources.

Later in Chapter 11, I will describe concrete methods for creating successful user experience innovation around positive surprises. Then in Chapter 15, I'll talk about how to create innovation for your core tasks.

Negative surprises should be generally avoided, especially in the core interaction of the product. But negative surprises—also known as *pain points*—can provide a very tangible approach to creating successful user experiences. (See Chapter 8 for more on pain points.)

User Experience Applies to Everything

User experience can be applied to almost all kinds of businesses. The user experience may seriously influence your brand, customer loyalty, and the amount of new customers considerably. Hence, it makes sense to take user experience very seriously for any kind of business.

For example, customers certainly get an impression of and feelings about a train company (Figure 1-9) if they have to wait 20 minutes in line to buy a train ticket, or if the trains are delayed frequently.

Figure 1-9. Example of user experience when purchasing train tickets

Likewise, customers will remember the atmosphere, interior, staff, waiting times, and service when using a bank. And people will certainly have good and bad experiences when they use a product or visit a web page.

People rarely use strong words such as *love* and *hate* about a product, but I am sure that there are hundreds of thousands of people in the world that would say that they love their social network service. You will also find thousands of people who love their iPhone, their Android product or similar, or even their bank. Finally, I am sure we have all hated our computer or a specific program when it crashes and decides to throw away the data you've been working on for the last two hours.

As mentioned, however, this book will focus mainly on how to create successful user experience innovations for devices, web pages, software, systems, and the like. But the book may still be good inspiration for organizations or companies who want to design a new shop interior layout, a better consumer experience when buying train tickets at the train station, and so on.

Summary

User experience is in my definition the changing *feelings* that a user gets when using a device, service, or system. User experience can come from a first impression. It can also come from positive and negative surprises experienced in the long term.

The ideal user experience is when the user—most of the time—feels happy, satisfied, proud, or even in love.

The ideal user experience can be achieved by knowing your target users and their needs, by focusing your design around core tasks, and by adding small positive surprises—in particular in the core interaction of your device.

User experience covers many disciplines and functions in a company. It is about unpredictable users' unpredictable feelings, and it covers basically any business. It's no wonder that many—especially smaller—companies give up even before considering improving the user experience.

The remainder of this book will hopefully bring user experience innovation from a complex academic level to a tangible level. Creating great user experiences does not require a master's degree, but it does require some practical tools and methods.

Innovating in User Experience

2

The first chapter briefly introduced you to what user experience is about, but the core scope of this book is how to *create* successful innovations within the area of user experience. This chapter describes the basics of how to achieve successful user experience innovation.

The Three Levels

I distinguish between three levels of innovation in user experience: *creativity, innovation,* and *success.* Success might seem like a strange choice, but it is important. Innovation without successful implementation is of little use and will not create products that create positive feelings for the user.

Creativity

Creativity is the ability to come up with ideas. Basically *any* ideas. They can be new, they can have been used before in another context, and they can be copied and adapted from a directly competing device. Figure 2-1 illustrates how the creative mind might work. There is a lot of chaos, but also a lot of raw material to work from.

Creativity can be a gift granted to specific persons, but in most cases creativity is solely about using the right approach, having the right mindset, and using the right tools. Creativity is merely the ability to create an idea, without necessarily taking into account whether the idea covers any user need or can be implemented with currently available technology. Creativity itself will hence rarely make your product successful. Innovation is also needed.

Figure 2-1. Creativity

Innovation

The majority of ideas created by teams or individuals in companies and organizations rarely make it to the market. My definition of *innovation* is to bring an idea to the market. This means that the term *innovation* automatically includes that the idea can be implemented with currently available technologies and resources.

However, bringing an idea to the market does not necessarily mean that the innovation will be successful. Many innovations are never or rarely used, and these innovations will hence typically not provide any benefit (e.g., profit) for the company or organization bringing them out. The most common—and saddest—case is that the innovation is not even noticed; not by analysts, not by magazines, and not by the consumers.

This tragedy of failed innovation often happens when a company launches a new technology that the user may feel sounds *cool*, but the company forgets to provide any valuable methods to use this new technology. Technology in itself very rarely sells any products.

It also happens that companies actually design methods of using the new technology, but the users see no need for the functionality. Or a company may fail to design the functionality with an adequate user experience that makes users realize a need for the technology. Figure 2-2 shows an example of a clear innovation—combining an orange with a kiwi—but one that has no obvious user need (at least for me).

Figure 2-2. Example of innovation with no (proven) user need

Throughout the history of mobile phones and devices, there have been a large number of failed innovations where technology has been sold as the next great thing, but where either the implementation was not adequate or where the users did not see the need (examples are Wireless Application Protocol [WAP] and push-to-talk [PTT]). Your technology—or rather the solutions you design for your technology—has to cover an existing, perceived, or latent user need.

By launching a good idea too early, by designing it with an insufficient user experience, by hiding it deep within menus, and so on, you may be wasting a lot of resources when developing your product and bringing your idea to the market, and you may also be opening a door for your competitors to copy your idea—and to design it *right*.

Success

Successful innovation is when a new (or old) idea is brought to the market that the markets, analysts, magazines, and most importantly, the *users* perceive as innovative. Analysts and magazines may sometimes see it as successful innovation when you simply bring a new technology or idea to the market. However, the customers who pay your salary in the end are not so easy to trick. If they not do perceive or feel any value or relevance for your new technology, then you do not have a successful user experience innovation. Successful user experience innovation is when your *users* acknowledge and appreciate your ideas, and when *they* see them as innovative.

Successful user experience innovation happens when the users feel that the innovation gives *true value* and is *relevant* for them. Hence, it comes back to the needs of the user. If the user *feels* that the innovation is relevant, cool, or amazing, then you may have created a successful user experience innovation.

Most ideas are not new. Many innovations are not new either. But the company that manages to bring an idea to the market first with the *right user experience* is often seen as the real inventor of the idea. And the idea is seen as truly novel. History writers and users generally only remember the companies that did a new technology *right*, not the companies that did it first.

Anecdote

Did Apple invent the finger touch–enabled smart phone? No. But Apple was the first to make it with a good user experience. And therefore it became successful. Of course, the Apple brand and some other elements added to the success—but keep in mind that the success of the Apple brand comes not least from the user experience of Apple's previous products.

Characteristics of Successful User Experience Innovation

Successful user experience innovation will make your consumer say "wow." It will make your consumer smile, or it will make your consumer think, "This is clever," or "What a positive surprise." Success will only happen, however, if the user sees your solution, product, or service as relevant. Without need, there is no success.

Another equally important, but much subtler, thought that users may have when operating your successful user experience innovation is, "This just works," or "I got my task done." They may not know why they feel this, they may not know all the intelligent user experience design and technologies that enabled this almost seamless interaction, but they just feel in control and comfortable.

These feelings inside the user do not need to be strong—at least not all the time—but they should be there. They should be there when using the product the first time, when using the product longer term, when upgrading the product, and so forth.

Figure 2-3 shows the five main characteristics of a successful user experience innovation:

- Relevance
- Positive feelings or wow
- Perception of uniqueness or novelty
- Visibility
- Marketability

Figure 2-3. The five main elements of successful user experience innovation

Relevance

Relevance indicates that the user experience innovation you create is covering a real or latent need of the end users. Without need, the user experience innovation will not be successful.

Positive Feelings

A successful user experience innovation makes the user feel happy, satisfied, confident, comfortable, or positively surprised, and it may even give the user a wow experience with your product. Ideally, you want your users to love your product and the experience it gives.

To trigger positive feelings with the user, your design needs to be inviting, simple, and focused. Negative feelings should always be avoided, and the causes of these feelings (usually pain points) should be eliminated. Several of the methods described later in this book help you to achieve positive feelings for the end user.

Uniqueness or Novelty

A successful user experience innovation is perceived as novel and unique. The technologies, applications, and solutions you use to generate that perception may not be new at all, but what counts is the perception of the end users, not so much the reality of the situation.

For example, many people perceived the iPod as the first MP3 player. It's easy to do research and prove otherwise, but for many people the iPod was the first MP3 player they had ever heard of, and so was born the perception that the iPod was new and unique.

Visibility

You want to place your user experience innovation where a majority of your target users will experience it (e.g., in the core tasks of your product). User experience innovation placed in rarely visited corners of your product may give a small positive surprise when found, but it will rarely make your overall product successful.

In some cases, successful user experience innovation is done in a hidden way. Maybe you have designed underlying intelligence that guesses what the user wants, and the user will consequently—if the product is designed right—be left with a positive feeling that "it just works." However, since the user still notices that the product "just works," this innovation can hardly be called invisible.

In other words, innovation needs to be visible. Otherwise hardly anyone will ever see it, and hence it cannot be seen as an innovation.

Marketability

Successful user experience innovations can often be used in marketing campaigns. If your user experience is great, then it is difficult to find better ways to market your product than through these user experience innovations.

Anecdote

Many mobile phones have simple designs, like the one in Figure 2-4, and are specifically sold based on their simple user experience. The same goes for a number of other products, including systems, software packages, and electronic devices of all sorts.

Figure 2-4. A mobile phone designed around a simple user experience

The Value of User Experience Innovation

The value of user experience innovation is threefold:

- Successful user experience innovations will make your product *stand out* from the competition. The customers will most likely prefer your solution and product.

- User experience will become the *key battlefield* for competition in the future, and it already is the main battle ground in many current areas.

- User experience innovation is and will continue to be the main *brand-building* tool.

Anecdote

Nokia used to rule the mobile device industry and was seen as the absolute innovation leader in the mobile phone industry. It was famous for its superior user experiences, but at a certain point the market and consumers began to lack new and valuable user experience innovations from Nokia.

What made customers switch from traditional keypad-based mobile phones to finger touch–operated smart phones? Was it the technology itself? Definitely not, since the technology was available on devices more than ten years before Apple reinvented it for the iPhone. It was even available on devices from top-branded mobile device manufacturers, so the Apple brand cannot account solely for the success either.

The answer is simple: Apple managed to create a user experience for finger-touch technology that customers saw a real value in. Users felt that the coolness and benefits of such a device were enough for them to start learning a completely new interaction paradigm. And Apple designed this interaction so cleverly that the transition was not hard at all.

Apple saw this sweet spot, and it created the iPhone with successful user experience innovation. Apple entered the market, and within a few years it basically took away the high-profit smart phone market from Nokia.

Does Innovation Conflict with Good User Experience?

When operating a product (a software program, a device, a web page, or similar), users may be reluctant to face radical innovation and changes in the interaction paradigm. When users buy a new product, they often feel most comfortable when they feel familiarity and can operate the product from day one.

So one could argue that innovation is in conflict with good user experience. However, I disagree with this. Instead I believe that user experience will become the key tool for most innovation in the future—whether it's the experience you get in your jewellery shop, or the one you get for devices, web pages, software programs, and so forth.

Yes, new technologies will continuously appear and mature, but technology innovations alone do not make successful innovation. The user experience and the clever ideas around the technology are what give users value, and this value is what will make successful innovations.

Innovation for the sake of innovation is seldom successful. Users need to feel a true (real or potential) value to change their habits and to learn new interactions. Consider for a moment the gas and brake pedals in a car (Figure 2-5).

Figure 2-5. What if we swap the gas and brake pedals?

Let us for example assume that a car manufacturer decides to swap the brake pedal with the gas pedal. The car manufacturer may have found out that it would give a better-looking visual design and a long-term ergonomic improvement. This is certainly an innovation, and studies and tests may even support that the user experience would be better in the long run. But obviously swapping the gas and brake pedals would never be a successful innovation. The swap would require too much for users to adapt to. Users would feel no incentive to learn this new interaction because they would not see a real value.

If a car manufacturer instead totally redesigned a car to give it lots of real value and novel functionality, the innovation *might* be successful. One such successful example was when cars began to come with automatic gear shifters instead of manual ones. The benefits were obvious and for most users desirable, and hence users wanted to adapt to this new technology.

Therefore, if you bring *real* (perceived or true) value to a product that users think is *relevant,* then you may be able to create even a radical innovation that is successful.

But innovation in itself is in no way conflicting with user experience. In fact, I would claim that in the near future, most innovation will be focused purely on the user experience. In other words, user experience will be (and already is) the *main tool for innovation* for devices, web pages, software programs, shopping experiences, and basically any other experience you can think of.

Summary

This chapter defined and explained key elements needed for successful user experience innovation, including what it is, what characterizes it, and what its value is. Subsequent chapters will provide tangible methods for creating successful user experience innovations.

CHAPTER

Identifying Target Users

3

For all of the innovation methods described in this book, it is essential to identify the end-user needs, which for simplicity I will call *user needs*. However, before you can find out the user needs, you will need to identify and define who your target users are.

Defining New Target Users

If your company already has a successful social website for teenagers, but you want to create a similar website for other users, you may need to start defining who the target users should be. Should your website be for elderly people looking to talk to their grandchildren? Or should you instead focus on tweens? Or should you create a social website for exotic butterfly enthusiasts? You may have several possible groups in mind, as illustrated in Figure 3-1, but your goal should generally be to narrow this down to just one group, or at least a few groups that are related.

Figure 3-1. Defining a new target user group

If you have a start-up company, you'll probably already have certain target users in mind when you start creating your first product, but it is still worth considering other target users from the beginning.

Having multiple target user groups may be a big advantage for some types of products. However, targeting multiple groups also has some pitfalls. You can't always please multiple groups at the same time.

How to find specific new groups of users to target is out of the scope of this book, and will depend on a variety of factors, including the current competition, the nature of your product(s), and the disposable income of the different groups you are targeting.

Larger companies often use internal or external market research to identify new potential target users. Smaller companies may lack the resources for extensive market research, but may have intrinsic insight into markets that can be profitably targeted. One thing, though, is for sure: you need to thoroughly investigate the market to find out who the potential target users for your product are.

Some companies tend to automatically choose target groups that are similar to their current user base. This can be a safe choice in some situations. In other situations, this sort of inward focus may cause a high risk of overlooking great opportunities with completely different target user groups.

Targeting a Predefined User Group

In large companies, user experience designers are often given a specific target user group as the starting point for the innovation work. Mature adults with a relatively large disposable income is an example of such a predefined group. You will often want to display these users with a representative photo, like in Figure 3-2, before continuing your work. A photo of your typical target users can help you a lot in the proceeding steps.

Depending on the quality of the market research, the research material may also contain a number of insights for the predefined group of users that you are targeting. This research may even specify end-user needs.

However, in almost all most cases, you will want to find, interview, and get to know your target users better. This is because innovation is much easier when you have faced the target users than it is when you solely base your innovation on market research data and statistics. Even when needs are well defined by current research, you are well advised not to skip the interviewing process. After all, data and statistics can take you only so far.

Figure 3-2. Example of predefined target users

Determining the Group Size

Your target user group should be wide enough to make your product interesting for enough users so that you believe that your product can be profitable. How large a target user group should be will depend on your product, the target users, and the market situation.

Figure 3-3 illustrates the choice between a small and a large group. If you are designing a web page for customers in low-income countries, you may need millions of customers to make your business profitable. If you design a mobile device for oil billionaires, you may not need any more than ten customers for your product if you can achieve enough profit from each device.

Figure 3-3. Narrow or wide target user group?

At the same time, you generally want to keep your target user group as narrow as possible. Creating user experience innovation that will be successful for several millions of very different people is impossible. The reason is that you will end up spreading your focus and innovations too much. And you may also end up cluttering your user experience with hundreds of functions and technologies in an attempt to satisfy everyone.

So you want the size of your target user group to be big enough for your product to become profitable. And you also want your target user group to be small enough to actually be able to trigger some potentially successful user experience innovation. Like the shoes in Figure 3-4, there is no one, correct size.

Figure 3-4. One size does not fit all

If the marketing department in your company has already defined a target user group, you will, as a user experience innovator, want to review and challenge their choices if you can identify obvious flaws in their decision. You will also want to dig into the research material that they have. If your marketing team has defined "the world" as the target user group, you should probably ask them to go back and redo the research they have done so far.

Designing for Multiple Target Groups

How do you design for multiple groups (Figure 3-5) while maintaining focus and not diluting your efforts to the point of failure? One approach is to define *one* core target group of users, but also keep a number of side target groups in mind during the innovation process. This will ensure that you do not limit your solutions too much. It may also make it much easier for you to later expand your target user group easily. Since you'll already know which other target users could become interested in your product if the solutions you offer are twisted a little bit, you can more easily adapt.

Figure 3-5. Multiple target user groups

For example, if you are designing a mobile phone for low-income consumers in entry markets, you should try from the beginning to imagine other markets—or rather other target users. Maybe a low-priced mobile phone will also nicely target the elderly in mature markets, or perhaps tweens in North America with low disposable incomes.

However, keep the focus mainly on your *core* target user group. If you, for example, try to define innovations and solutions for consumers in low-income markets, elderly people in mature markets, and tweens in North America all at once, you will most likely fail. In most cases, you should keep your focus in all innovations on your core target users, but keep your secondary target users in mind also.

Sometimes you will realize that there are overlapping needs and solutions among your target user groups. If this is the case, you may be able to create solutions that apply to many more people than originally targeted. You may, for example, find out that both elderly people in mature markets and low-income users in entry markets (who may not be able to afford reading glasses) may need large fonts on mobile phone displays to make the text readable.

But in cases where the needs are conflicting, you should always prioritize your core target users. Tweens in North America may, for example, want as many functions and as much information as possible displayed at once, whereas your core target users in low-income markets may have the opposite need.

Anecdote

Facebook was originally designed and intended only for students at Harvard University. Only later was it extended to other colleges in the Boston area, and then beyond.

Today, Facebook has more than 800 million active users.[1] Facebook is hence a brilliant example of a product that was originally defined for a very narrow group of target users, but for which other potential target user groups were considered at an early stage.

Summary

Defining who your target users are is an essential step, since it will not only help you focus your innovations, your approach, and your marketing, but it will help you avoid creating a product that tries (and fails) to do everything for everyone.

Many products in this world were designed without specific customers in mind, and this is usually reflected in the lack of success of these products.

The conclusion is that defining—or identifying—your target users is a fine balance between using a small enough target user group to spark innovation, and at the same time defining a big enough target user group to allow for future growth.

---

[1] http://en.wikipedia.org/wiki/Facebook

Identifying User Needs

4

User needs are the cornerstones of all successful user experience innovation. If your product, solution, or functionality does not cover existing or latent needs of the target users, then all your efforts in creating a great user experience for this solution may well be wasted. In other words, *your user experience innovation will never be successful unless you cover an existing or latent end-user need.*

If you create a device that end users do not need, it will not sell. If you design a function for your word-processing software that users do not need, that function will never be used. If you create functionality or services on your web page that the user does not see any value or need for, these will not be used.

This may sound very logical, but it is amazing to see how many (unsuccessful) products and solutions are launched every year for which there is no or very limited user need. If you are adding functionality with no underlying user needs, you may not only be wasting resources on developing this functionality, but you may be decreasing the overall user experience of your product, simply because more functions generally mean decreased usability.

User Needs vs. Fundamental Human Needs

Researchers recognize a fairly well-defined set of fundamental human needs. These include the need for affection, for leisure, for protection. You would seldom use these human needs directly as the starting point for your innovation, even though in some cases and for some products such needs may be relevant.

Instead, you want user needs expressed as more tangible desires (Figure 4-1), wishes, or even dreams for your specific product. And you want your user needs to already be specific for your target users, reflecting cultural and human differences.

In many cases you can actually relate user needs directly back to fundamental human needs like protection, creation, identity, freedom, and so on. In the example in Figure 4-1 the underlying fundamental human need is clearly about safety and protection or even survival.

I want a function on the device that will help me if I get robbed when walking on the street at night

Figure 4-1. Example of a user need

User Needs vs. Core Tasks

User needs should also not be confused with core tasks, even though there is some resemblance. Core tasks are specific tasks that the user is already performing or expects to perform, whereas user needs express an existing or latent need related to a product. I would hence define the difference as follows: a user need may *lead* certain tasks to become core tasks over time, but never vice versa.

It is possible to innovate around core tasks, however. You'll read more about how to do that in Chapter 6.

Types of User Needs

I usually distinguish between three types of user needs: immediate user needs, perceived user needs, and latent user needs. These three types of user needs are briefly introduced next.

Immediate User Needs

Immediate user needs are the needs that users have here and now, and that most users can imagine and articulate. An example is, "I want this device to improve the safety of my family." Another example might be, "I want a device to inflate my bicycle tire."

Existing user needs also very much reflect user expectations. For example, a user visiting a site perceived as a social networking site might state, "I expect this web page to help me get in contact with my friends."

Immediate user needs are important to fulfill—for example, when selling a product or when users have just entered a certain web page and they are considering whether to spend more time on that page. Immediate user needs are, however, often a bit transient. They can change easily and rapidly. A user's immediate need for Facebook, for example, might change from posting entertaining photos one day to sending a serious note to a relative in the hospital the next.

Perceived User Needs

Perceived user needs are different from immediate user needs. Perceived user needs refer to tasks that the users—falsely—expect your product to solve. Perceived user needs are often superficial and created by hype in the market, or by marketing campaigns that make users believe they have a need for a certain product when they truly don't. Marketing alone does not, however, ensure a successful user experience.

So be careful with these needs. They may set the user's expectations too high, which can ruin both the first impression of your product and the long-term user experience.

The term *perceived value* should not be mixed up with the term *perceived user need*. Perceived value is certainly something to aim for, since it reflects that the user actually *does* see a value (be it illogical or real). On the other hand, a perceived need is often a superficial user feeling, which can lead you down the wrong track when innovating for user experiences.

Anecdote

When the first Internet-enabled mobile phones were introduced using the WAP standard, the industry, analysts, magazines, and marketing campaigns hyped this new technology to extreme heights. What happened after the launch of these devices was foreseeable for a user experience expert, but the results were devastating.

People expected a real Internet browser, and instead they got a very simple and expensive Internet connection with almost no web pages to visit. Luckily, consumers liked some of the first devices, such as the Nokia 7110 (shown in Figure 4-2), for other reasons—for example, the slide-out mouthpiece, the big display, the roller key, and so on.

Figure 4-2. The Nokia 7110; the first WAP-enabled mobile phone. Copyright Nokia 2011. Used by permission.

Latent User Needs

The term *latent user needs* covers in my definition both needs that the user already has but cannot imagine or articulate, and needs that the user may not even have yet. Latent needs can often be identified by observing the users of your product. Imagine that you are observing a user who is using your e-mail application, and you see him try to retype the content of the e-mail into a calendar reminder. The user may not be able to imagine easy solutions for moving the text over to the calendar, and hence he cannot express the need for a function to make that task easier. But you as the observer can easily identify the perceived need (see Figure 4-3).

Figure 4-3. Example of a latent user need

A latent need for parents might be a device or web page that allows them to see the exact location of their children (this may not, however, be a need for the children). But if the users can't imagine that this may actually be possible, it won't be expressed as a need.

Hydration packs represent an excellent example of a latent need translated into a successful product. Hikers, cyclists, skiers, and other outdoor enthusiasts have a need for water. Yet by and large, no one had been asking for a way to carry a bag of water on their back until the creators first saw the latent need, and then worked tirelessly to help others see it also. The result is that one hardly sees an outdoor sports enthusiast today who isn't carrying a bag of water.

A great visual or industrial design of your device or a surprising *wow*—function in your software package may also meet latent needs for beauty, joy, and surprise. If you, for example, buy a car and later realize that it can parallel-park automatically, you may be extremely satisfied with your car for covering a need that you would never have thought to express directly.

Note Don't think that you can avoid worrying about latent needs when designing tools that people are required to use in their work. The doctor who buys an iPhone will soon come to demand similar usability and joy from the products used in his medical practice.

Latent needs will almost never be expressed by the user (except maybe for a few lead users; see chapter 13), and can hence only be captured by observers who specifically look for them. Observers such as user experience experts hence must develop skill in detecting underlying needs during interviews, observation, and sometimes even usability tests.

Latent needs are crucial for user experience innovation, since they can often put you one step ahead of competition. Using feedback from customers is becoming quite common, but often that feedback is mainly used to fix pain points, as described in Chapter 9. Trying to look ahead—or into the underlying latent needs of customers—is still not common, and doing so may thus give you a competitive edge in your current market situation.

Remember that growth in almost all consumer-oriented industries does not come from lowering the cost of your products, but from creating great experiences when your users are using your products. A great user experience can create a tremendous value in a product. In today's economy, cost is certainly still important, but if you provide the user with a great experience (e.g., feeling), you can charge almost anything for your product.

My editor on this book purchased his first-ever mountain bike in 2002 for what seemed to him the extravagant sum of $350. Four years later, in fall of 2006, his dealer loaned him a full-suspension bike for the weekend. The loan of that bike awakened a latent need, and in spring of 2007 my editor spent $3,300 on a high-end suspension bike—almost ten times what he originally believed to be an extravagant price. He rides more and is now fitter than he has been in a decade. What made the difference? It was the fantastic user experience from the higher-end bike.

Interview your users. Observe them. Carefully consider their actions and whether any of those actions represent latent needs that can be addressed by creative solutions in and surrounding your products. Several of the user experience innovation methods in the remainder of this book will give concrete guidance on how to innovate for latent user needs.

Approaches to Identifying Needs

Assuming you already have a good understanding of who your target users are, which you should have from Chapter 3, the next step is to identify the needs of these users. There are many well-documented methods for identifying the needs of your target users; I will go through some of these methods in the sections to follow.

Finding Specific Target Users

Finding target users may sometimes be a little bit tricky. For example, if you are looking for tweens in your own market area, you can probably easily find some simply by walking the streets near your office or home. If your target users are people interested in butterflies from southern Borneo, you may want to try searching the Internet for potential existing butterfly or insect communities. If you are looking for tweens also interested in butterflies from southern Borneo, you are probably defining your target group to be too narrow.

If you are designing a product similar to what you already have on the market, you can look in your current database of customers, and you can browse through your consumer complaint database if you have one, or ask some colleagues working with customer feedback on a daily basis.

In some situations where you are looking for very specific user profiles, you may want to ask an agency to find suitable target users for you. Asking these agencies purely for names and addresses of specific types of users usually does not cost a fortune.

If you are targeting users that you have not been in contact with before, you may get more inspiration from Chapter 15, where I will go through the entire user experience innovation process for a product targeted at a new user group.

Contacting Target Users

The next step is to make initial contact with your target users. This can be done via e-mail or telephone, or by spotting them on the street. You will often be very surprised at how willing users will be to help you. They may sometimes happily take time off from their job to meet up with you for a few hours. You can contact some of your target users and ask them in for a session, or simply interview them via phone. E-mail interviews and web surveys may also be options, but—as mentioned later— these methods are less reliable.

Talking to Your Target Users

Talking to your target users may sound so obvious that it is not worth mentioning. However, you'd be surprised at the number of companies that omit this step. It is vital to actually talk to your target users.

Many companies do not even use existing feedback channels when they create new innovation. Most companies already have several ways to relate to their end users, such as e-mail inquiries and complaints, help lines, and so on, but these media are in many cases only used to give relief to users' frustrations. They are seldom used in the innovation process.

Don't fall into the trap of thinking that you must hire a research company to perform extensive and expensive market research. Doing so may be fruitful for larger companies. But if your resources are sparse, you can do research yourself very easily. Finding user insights is in my mind the absolute most prominent source of successful user experience innovation, so you certainly don't want to leave out the vital task of actually talking to your target audience.

In the following sections I will go through some of the methods of determining end-user needs that I personally have found most fruitful for sparking great innovations.

Interviewing Users or Potential Users

As indicated, talking to your users or potential users is essential. An alternative is a more formal way of interviewing people about their use of your product. This can bring you a number of insights and alert you to end-user needs. Interviewing people will sometimes automatically make the people more positive. It is very difficult for users to express negative elements of your product when interviewed, especially if you use a video or sound recorder. You see the same thing when a person from a political party interviews or questions people on the street.

The trick is to read behind the person, and to read what the person really means. They may tell you initially that your product is the best in the world, but try to listen to what they say after that. For example, they might say, "I love your product, but when I need to create a calendar reminder, I have some difficulties." The trick is to listen to everything that comes after the "but." You should also try to understand the basic needs of the person. This is usually where you will find true sources for later innovation around the user experience. If a person says to you that they love your product, but that they care more about the safety of their family, maybe the last part is where you should pay attention.

You can stop and interview people on the street, you can e-mail some of your users from your existing customer base, you can invite some specific users to a workshop, you can do web surveys, and you can interview people in their homes (see Figure 4-4).

Figure 4-4. Example of interviewing a target users in their home

Which method to choose may depend on the product that you are designing, and it will depend on the target users. Here are some examples:

- If you are designing a TV remote control, you might want to interview people in their homes so that they can show how they usually use your device in the place where they use it.

- If you are designing a web page, service, or device for physically challenged users, you will likewise want to visit them in the place where they use your product.

- If you are designing a web page for teenagers, you may want to visit the teenagers in their rooms, in an Internet café, or wherever they most typically would use your product.

- If you are designing a mobile phone, asking people on the street may be suitable if the scope of your innovation is something that they would use when walking on the street.

The method you use for your interviews is for your discretion and judgement based on the product you are designing. But keep in mind that the goal of your interview is to find existing or latent needs.

During my time with Nokia, I organized and participated in a large number of creative workshops. I participated with people from different disciplines of R&D, as well as from marketing, product planning, and management.

You may often experience that people attending a workshop will bring predefined opinions, solutions, and ideas. A very good way to reset—or rather to focus—the participants minds at the start of a creative workshop is by asking the people to perform street interviews for a few hours. Simply ask your participants to stop people walking on the street and ask about needs for your product.

Performing street interviews may not necessarily give you a huge number of new insights, but it may certainly give your participants a renewed view on your product and why innovation is needed. Insights found by people themselves tend to be much more influential than those found by reports from a market research agency.

However, whether you choose street interviews, phone interviews, e-mail interviews, web surveys, market research, or a combination will depend on the complexity of your product and the target users.

Empathic Design

Emphatic design is a variation of user observation. With this technique, you as the observer look for underlying feelings to identify latent user needs.[1] In many ways, empathic design is a matter of *how* you observe users. It takes some practice to see beyond the obvious user needs to the latent needs, but with a little bit of practice most people can do it. Alternatively, you may want to use a professional user experience expert to help you out.

When you start learning to see latent needs, you will automatically start to see latent needs when you observe people in public—on trains, buses, the street, and other places. You will be surprised about what insights and latent user needs you can find this way.

In 1999 I was sitting on a train on the way back home from work. I couldn't help observing a teenage girl using her mobile phone. She was writing texts at high speed, and the constant sound of incoming messages told me that she was also receiving many messages. I ended up saying out loud that she certainly had many friends, and to my surprise she said that she was only communicating with a single person, her best friend.

---

[1] For more information on empathic design, see http://en.wikipedia.org/wiki/Empathic_design.

At this time in mobile phone history, mobile phones had no conversational SMS reading view, so when she received a new message from her friend, she would have to exit the writing of the current message, go to standby mode, read the new message received, and return to the text editor to continue writing her message. I concluded from this that this specific user had a latent need for a method where SMS communication with a single user was much easier than what was the case at that time.

The next day at work I designed—and patented[2]—the first ever chat function for a mobile phone, the so-called SMS Chat feature (Figure 4-5). Of course, this insight needed a lot more verification and selling inside the company, but the SMS Chat feature was developed and launched in 2000 for one of the most successful mobile devices ever, the Nokia 3310.[3]

Figure 4-5. The original version of SMS Chat for the Nokia 3310

The SMS Chat feature ended up as one of the key unique selling points of the 3310,[4] and you will still find an unmodified version of this function in low-cost mobiles from Nokia. You will also find this same functionality in modernized versions on Nokia devices, iPhones, and so on.

Market Research

Market research is basically no different from stopping and interviewing users on the street. However, you may not have time to interview hundreds of users and generate statistical data based on the interviews. You also may not have the same experience in interviewing users as professional agencies have. Finally, you may not have the time to do it yourself.

In this case, having professional market research done may be an option. It will surely cost you more money, but you may in return get data that is more precise, better documented, and covers more users than what you could have generated yourself. Interviewing random people on the street may give you very good inspira-

---

[2] See, e.g., patent US6915138

[3] http://en.wikipedia.org/wiki/Nokia_3310

[4] http://asia.cnet.com/reviews/mobilephones/0,39051200,10000370p,00.htm

tion for what a specific user wants, but market research may give you much more precise data about the users you are targeting.

Market research can provide you with more precise data about the needs of your target users, but it may take longer, and it won't give you the hands-on experience that in itself can be a great source of inspiration for user experience innovation.

Note If you already have good market research data, I still recommend trying out, for example, simple street interviews—not because the experience of interviewing people on the street will necessarily give you better data, but because it is a great source of innovation.

A Day in the Life

If the product that you are designing will have many contact points with the user during a day, you may choose a *day-in-the-life* method (Figure 4-6). This is a practical approach in which you interview target users about a typical day in their life, and you can learn when and why they might choose your product to accomplish some of their daily tasks. You may also choose to follow a user throughout an entire day and simply take notes.

Figure 4-6. A day-in-the-life example

This approach may be applicable to social web pages, certain software programs such as word processors and e-mail clients, mobile phones, remote controls, and so forth. If your product does not naturally have many contact points during a day, you might change this to a week-in-the-life or a month-in-the-life exercise.

Not only will this exercise provide you with specific, immediate end-user needs for your product, but it may also provide you with indirectly expressed latent user needs. If you can convince the user to let you take photos during the day, you will get a lot of concrete footage and inspiration for the succeeding innovation work.

Furthermore, this exercise may give you indications of the what the user's core tasks are (see Chapter 5), as well as the current pain points that the user is experiencing (see Chapter 9).

User-Created Diaries

Another approach to finding user needs is to ask target users to create diaries about their life, and about how, when, and where they use your product (see Figure 4-7).

Figure 4-7. User-created diaries

Several agencies specialize in finding users that match your target user group. These users are more than willing to create loads of diary material—and hence end-user needs—for a relatively small sum of money. In some cases, giving these users one of your products may be enough.

> **Note** Remember that if you have customers that truly like your product already, these customers may be willing to go a long way for you. Use that. And use their expertise.

Lead User Workshops

Most of the target users for your product will have difficulties expressing their needs for your product. And a vast majority of your target users will certainly not be able to come up with the innovations themselves. There will always be some users who are exceptions, though—those who are leaders and trend setters. These are the *lead users* of your product, and they are the ones you should seek out and bring into a workshop (Figure 4-8).

Figure 4-8. A user workshop

If you are designing a web page, you might look for users who are already making additions or modifications to your web page. If you are designing slide presentation software, you will be looking at the people who are already creating Visual Basic plug-ins for your software. If you are designing a mobile phone, you will be looking for users who are already writing their own applications or tweaking the software. If you are designing a TV remote control, you may want to look for users who disassemble your unit and make their own modifications.

Lead users may not necessarily represent the needs of your typical target users, since they sometimes have niche needs that are not common for your overall target user group, but these users can be valuable in many other ways. In Chapter 13 I will describe how to create innovations *together* with lead users.

Rules for Interviewing End Users

You and your colleagues may not be used to stopping people on the street to interview them. You may not be used to entering their homes. A few dos and don'ts are needed if you choose to approach your target users yourself.

You can find numerous articles, books, and blogs on the subject of interviewing. Here I will just emphasize a few key guidelines. Most of the benefit will come from the few guidelines I list here.

- Do not ask leading questions to users, such as, "Do you want gears on your bicycle?" They will most likely say yes no matter what they think. Ask open-ended questions instead, such as, "What problems do you encounter when pedalling over changing terrain?"

- Try to get under the skin of the users. Try to find out their current and latent needs. Ask them about their typical behavior when they use your or related products.

- Do not ask users only product-related questions. Try to find out who they are and be open and be ready for long stories about their life. Being honestly interested in people and their lives will not only help those people to open up and give you better insights, but it will help their stories sometimes become the core source of new innovations that you wouldn't otherwise think about.

- Do not use fancy equipment such as recorders and video cameras unless you already have agreed on this with the users. Also, keep in mind that what people say to a camera or a recorder will be very biased compared to what they will say in a casual conversation. When you finish the interview, you can ask if you can take a single photo of the person you interviewed. This photo will be very useful for you later when documenting the user needs for that specific person.

Be open, be honest, and be humble. Avoid being perceived as confrontational. It's so easy for an interview to go off the rails, as depicted in Figure 4-9. Open-ended questions, willingness to listen, and genuine interest go a long way toward avoiding interview failure.

Figure 4-9. Interview gone wrong

Documenting User Needs

Filtering data from a large amount of user interviews may take some time, unless you use the easy (but still relevant) method of asking only very few users. When you have found the core needs of your target users, you need to document these needs for the user experience innovation.

You can record your findings by showing the user needs expressed as specific statements from the persons that you interviewed—with the photo of the person in the middle. Figure 4-10 shows an example, listing needs of a mobile phone intended for low-income consumers in emerging markets.

If you have very extensive user data and want to compress it, you may need to invent a *typical person* for your user need statements. However, you should have a professional researcher do this to avoid too much personal bias.

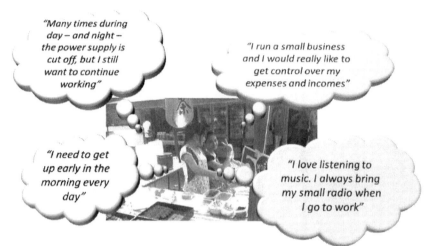

Figure 4-10. One method for showing the needs of target users

Summary

This chapter has provided you with tangible methods to find the user needs for your target users. The user needs of your target users are the base for all successful user experience innovation.

Identifying Core Tasks

5

The last chapter gave you methods to find user needs. User needs are in some cases directly useful for user experience innovation. Usually though, you first of all want to find out what the user would like to *achieve* with your product. What are the tasks that the user is already achieving or desires to achieve with your product? Which tasks would the user like to use your product for in the future? These are key questions to answer. Identifying current and future potential core tasks for your product makes it much easier for you to identify which applications or features you will need to focus on in the product development.

Core task is often mistakenly used as a synonym for *application* or *feature*, but the terms mean different things. A core task is something that the user *wants* to achieve. A core task is hence purely focused around the user.

Feature and *application* are terms invented by designers and engineers to describe a piece of software or hardware. A feature or application may—or may not—help the user to achieve her core task. Sometimes solving a core task will require two or more applications, and the user may use the same features or applications to solve several different core tasks.

If the user of a mobile phone wants to solve the core task of calling a friend, he may use several applications. For example, he may use the contacts list, the call-handling application, and the volume control application. If the user wants to solve the core task of answering a call, he may use several of the same applications as when making a call.

By identifying your target users' core tasks, you may not only identify that you are missing a number of features and applications, but you may also be able to identify which areas of your current product you need to focus your innovation around. Finally, you can also use your core tasks for identifying and innovating around pain points.

Characteristics of a Core Task

My definition of a core task is a task that a large number of end users would expect to be able to perform with a specific device, web page, or system.

A core task hence does *not* have to be a task that your users are already performing in your product. A core task can be a task that your users would *like* to perform, but where no solutions—or at least no adequate solutions—are yet available. A core task is hence any task that users *expect* to be able to perform with your product. It is important to emphasize that core tasks are *defined by the users*.

Here are some examples of wrong-headed thinking:

- When a company chooses to put stock information on its front page, it is in most cases not because a large number of users see viewing that information as a core task. It is more likely because the management sees it as the most important information to push to the users.

- When a web page initially wants to ask users 10 to 20 questions before proceeding to the actual content, it is most likely not because the users think it is essential.

- When a mobile device manufacturer chooses to force users to sign up for an account with its application store before even being able to make a phone call, it is not because the users see creating an account as a core task. It is more likely because the manufacturer wants to boost the amount of registered users on their application store.

However, when you choose to push irrelevant information and force users through tasks that they feel have no value, you will lose visitors to your web page, you will lose customers on your Internet store, you will get unsatisfied customers for your devices, and you will negatively impact the brand of your company.

Core Tasks Vary by Product

Core tasks are defined as the most desired functionalities of your web page, device, or system—in other words, the tasks that the end users would like to use in your product.

The core tasks will hence vary for different types of products, and here are few examples:

- A car key, such as in Figure 5-1, performs three core tasks: unlocking the doors, locking the doors, and starting the engine.

Figure 5-1. Car key

- For a TV remote control, you would probably see functions like powering on, powering off, and channel changing as core tasks. Also, adjusting volume and muting the TV would fall under core tasks. (Initial setting up of the TV channels is also a core task, even though it may be performed only one time).

- For a social community web page, core tasks may be changing your own status, seeing the status of your friends, inviting friends to events, sharing photos, and viewing photos.

Core Tasks Are Not Solutions

Core tasks are not solutions, features, or applications. They are tasks that the end user has a wish to accomplish. A core task is hence never a button, a menu, a touch screen, a Bluetooth chip, or a specific interaction flow. These things are merely solutions to help the user in solving a core task.

In the case of the remote control, you would hence not define the volume keys as a core task. The keys are nothing more than your specific solution to allow the users to accomplish core tasks (adjusting the volume, muting, etc.).

By seeing core tasks as what they are—*tasks*—you will realize how much innovation can be made around them.

Core Tasks Differ for Different Groups

Core tasks may vary depending on the individual user, or at least for different groups of target users. So for every new group of users that you choose to target, you will need to identify the core tasks again. And for every new target user group you will hence also need to look for new user experience innovations that are relevant to these users.

Core Tasks Link Back to User Needs

User needs often indirectly link back to the fundamental needs of human beings (food, safety, health, etc.), and hence these needs change slowly over time. User needs for a specific product are often defined as concrete wishes or desires, such as, "I need the product to provide safety for my family." The underlying fundamental human need (in this case, *safety*) is often quite visible, even when applied to specific products.

Core tasks also link back to the fundamental human needs, but core tasks will change when new technologies or applications are added to a product and when the users have learned the *new skills* required to master the new technology or application.

What Makes a Task Evolve into a Core Task?

Core tasks change more rapidly than user needs, since core tasks will change when new skills are learned by the user. Until around 1995, the core tasks of most mobile phones were making calls and receiving calls. After 1995, sending and receiving messages became core tasks for an increasing number of users. Despite the fact that the first mobile phones with Internet access and e-mail support were launched in the mid-1990s, browsing the Internet and writing/receiving e-mails did not become core tasks until much later (2005 or later).

Anecdote

The ability to send and receive texts on Global System for Mobile Communications (GSM) mobile phones was there almost from the very beginning, which means around 1990; it was part of the first GSM standards. Many devices supported this from the beginning of the 1990s, but almost no one in the industry saw any potential in this ability. Who would use a small keypad that was never designed for text writing to send messages (and that had room for only 160 characters)?

The operators had to invest in expensive SMS service centers, so they deliberately charged SMS sending accordingly. Initial cost for sending a single SMS message was up to $1.

According to Wikipedia,[1] SMS usage was around 0.4 messages sent per customer per month in 1995. Around 1998, a Norwegian GSM operator performed an experiment and made SMS sending free of charge for its customers. A few hours later, the SMS service centers handling the messages crashed due to overload.

This was a wake-up call for the entire mobile industry. Message sending was suddenly on everyone's lips and everybody realized that an important core task for mobile phone users had been overlooked for many years.

At Nokia, we immediately gathered a small team, with me as one of the lead designers. The target was to introduce T9 (predictive text input[2]) to a product that was almost ready to be launched. With a very tight schedule and impatient software developers and product managers breathing down our necks, we managed to introduce the first T9-enabled mobile phone in 1999—the very successful Nokia 3210.[3] See Figure 5-2 for an example of T9 input in action.

Figure 5-2. T9 text input

Today, a large number of mobile phone users see sending and receiving e-mails, browsing the Internet, playing games, taking photos, and GPS navigation as

[1] http://en.wikipedia.org/wiki/SMS

[2] http://en.wikipedia.org/wiki/T9_%28predictive_text%29

[3] http://en.wikipedia.org/wiki/Nokia_3210

core tasks of a mobile phone. What actually made these tasks become core tasks for the mobile phone users? Was there no need to access the Internet from your mobile phone back in 1995? Did people not have a need to use their mobile phone for capturing photos?

Part of the answer is that Internet access technologies, text-writing methods, camera units, and so on were neither mature nor cheap enough to be included on a mobile phone. Also, operator billing schemes and low Internet speed was a factor in the slow uptake.

But in my opinion, the main reason was that the user experience for these technologies was not made good enough until around 2005. User experience in this case includes interaction methods, screen resolutions, acceptable camera quality, fast Internet connections, and also acceptable operator billing plans.

Today many customers believe that the first mobile phone with Internet access and a browser was the iPhone, even though it came more than ten years after the first Internet-enabled mobile phones.

If you want a big impact for your product in the market, then you need to focus your innovation primarily on the core tasks that the users will perform on your system, device, or web page.

If you want to change an entire industry, you will want to identify potential and future core tasks of your product and then create a superb user experience for these core tasks in your product.

Time-Critical Core Tasks

Some core tasks have a different nature since they may be time critical. If, for example, your telephone starts ringing while you're watching TV, muting the TV will in this situation be a time-critical core task. And you may want to come up with an innovation such as shaking the remote control to quickly mute the TV.

Finding your mobile phone when a call is coming in is another example of a time-critical core task. When your phone rings, you often want to answer it before you miss the call.

Finding specific information on a company website is yet a third example of a time-critical core task, if you want to quickly look up specific data. The fact that many company websites do not support good solutions for this core task is one of the reasons for the success of Internet search engines, which can get you directly to the content you need on a company website, without your having to go through the maybe unintuitive front page of this company's website.

To some extent you may want to see all core tasks as time critical. With a few exceptions (such as game playing), users do not want to use excessive time completing a task. They want to complete most tasks as quickly as possible—and without problems. If a product competing with your product gets the core tasks done faster and more easily, then you may have a problem.

However, highly time-critical core tasks often need different solutions than other core tasks. In many cases, simple, intuitive, and fast solutions may be preferable.

Potential Future Core Tasks

Remember that some core tasks may not yet have been learned by the users. The users may already have the underlying need to perform a task with your product, but you or the entire industry may not yet have provided solutions that are good enough for the users to learn the new task. Such tasks represent possibilities for innovation.

Alternatively, you may as a company simply not be aware that an underlying need exists. The SMS anecdote earlier in this chapter is an example of such a case. Again, such needs are possibilities for innovation and profit.

Why Innovate Around Core Tasks?

Creating user experience innovation around your core tasks is essential for a web page, a device, or any other system. First of all, your core tasks are the tasks on which your users spend most of their time with your product, so this is an excellent place to give the users a little wow or provide them with a nice experience. Secondly, because your users spend most of their time and focus on the core tasks, they represent natural—and for the users, *expected*—areas in which to keep improving and innovating. Users will over time increase their expectations in exactly these areas.

By knowing your users' core tasks, you will also find it easier to prioritize improvements and resource spending in the future. You can focus resources primarily on core tasks and new innovations instead of fixing problems in areas that the customers never use.

Method for Identifying Core Tasks

This section describes a stepwise approach to identifying both the current and future potential core tasks of your product. In overview, the steps are as follows:

Step 1: Identify or Define Your Target Users

Step 2: Identify the User Needs of the Target Users

Step 3: Identify the Core Tasks of Your Product

Step 4: Identify Potential Future Core Tasks

Step 5: Document Your Preliminary Core Tasks

Step 6: Verify and Prioritize Your Core Tasks

Step 7: Identify the Top Core Tasks for Your Product

Step 8: Process and Document the Results

Step 1: Identify or Define Your Target Users

Since core tasks will change with user needs, which again will change with the target users you are approaching, identifying—or defining—your target users is the first essential step. Throughout this chapter, I will as an example use a music-playing device targeted for teenagers in developed markets (see Figure 5-3).

Figure 5-3. Target users in the example: teenagers in developed markets

Step 2: Identify the User Needs of the Target Users

You can use the methods described in the previous chapter to identify the user needs for the target users. For the music player example, we will assume that you have already identified the user needs of the teenagers in developed markets. Figure 5-4 shows a list of the user needs for teenagers in developed markets. The list is deliberately made incomplete to keep the example simple.

As the figure indicates, you do not want to limit the user needs to those specifically relevant to your current product or assumed product, and you certainly want to list needs that the users currently use other products or means to achieve. Several of these latent user needs can perhaps be achieved with the product you are designing, and you will hence have a unique chance to create the first product of its kind that solves these needs. You will in other words get almost direct inputs to ideas about where you can improve your product in the future and where you can add successful user experience innovation.

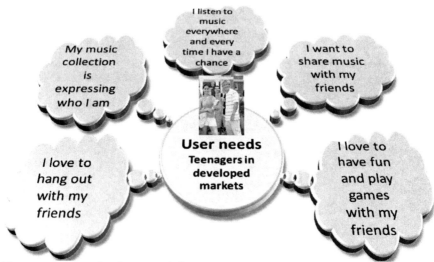

Figure 5-4. Example of user needs for teenagers in developed markets

Step 3: Identify the Core Tasks of Your Product

If you already have a similar product on the market for similar target users, you may be tempted to identify your current core tasks by asking your existing users what tasks they already perform. You could hold a meeting, such as in Figure 5-4.

If your product is a web page or a software application, you can run statistics on which tasks the users are performing with your product. These can give you information about which tasks are currently core for the current users.

Figure 5-5. Identifying core tasks

However, since core tasks are defined as tasks that the user *expects* to use your product for, your interviews and statistics will be skewed by how well you have designed the features or applications for your core tasks. If you have, for example, designed your calendar application for your web page very poorly or hidden it under some difficult-to-understand drop-down menu, your feedback and data may not highlight tasks such as creating appointments as core. Also, statistical data will also reveal tasks that you have not implemented yet.

Also, which is often the case, you may be targeting a different group of users with your new product. Hence your statistics and user interviews will be obsolete.

In some cases you may also look at your pain points. Pain points can, for example, be identified by going through e-mails or call logs from your customer service. Not only are pain points great tools for innovating user experience improvements (as described in Chapter 9), but they may also reveal the tasks that users are performing (or expecting to perform) a lot in your product.

While statistical data and pain points may sometimes be useful to identify existing core tasks, you will always want to back up your core task identification with the approach described following. Certain market research agencies will also be able to provide you with an approach similar to the one I describe. My approach, however, may be lower key and hence maybe easier to take.

Gathering a Group of Cross-Functional Team Members and Lead Users

The first thing you want to do is to invite cross-functional team members for a short innovation session. You want to invite team members from different parts of the company, especially those who specialize in user experience design and consumer insights. Who to invite from your company depends on the size and structure of your organization, as well as the type of product you are designing.

You should also ideally invite real users. Discovering core tasks by analyzing user needs will surely require interviewing actual users.

Process for Identifying Core Tasks for Your Product

My suggestion for this approach is to use a simple drawing (e.g., on a white board) where you place a photo of a representative target user—or multiple photos of target users—in the center, and then place the user needs around the user, basically as suggested already in Figure 5-5 for the music player example. You can use this drawing with the team of people you have gathered and start imagining which user tasks may be core tasks for *your* product.

Identifying core tasks for elements that you already have solutions for in your existing products is usually quite straightforward, since you know your products and can easily relate to these tasks. But a core purpose of this workshop is to also identify core tasks that are currently not covered by your product. These are the so-called future potential core tasks.

Again, you want to keep the type of product you are designing in mind, but do not be too restrictive. You need to try to imagine what kind of tasks the type of product you are designing may likely be used for in the future. It is essential to be innovative in this process; it's fine to come up with wild ideas for core tasks, since you will need to verify your core tasks with the target users later anyway.

You may also look at related products to get inspiration. If you are designing a music player, you might, for example, look at what is happening in the market for other handheld devices, such as mobile phones, navigation devices, portable game devices, and so on.

The result of the workshop could, for example, be as displayed as in Figure 5-6, which shows the results for the music player example.

Figure 5-6. Example of results from finding core tasks from user needs

Step 4: Identify Potential Future Core Tasks

You may have market research or other insights indicating a rising interest for solutions that your product is already offering, or that your product could offer in future. These tasks are hence not core tasks yet, but they may well become core tasks in the future.

Identifying potential future core tasks is extremely important, since there are many possibilities for successful user experience innovation if your product can provide solutions for these latent user needs before your competition will do it. For finding potential future core tasks, you need to identify latent or already existing user needs among your target users.

If you are designer of a company website, you will try to find out what information and applications are missing on your website. You want to look for ideas from customer feedback. You will check what competing companies offer on their web-sites. And you will want to interview customers about what they are missing and about their latent needs.

If you are designing a device, you will look at competitor devices to see if they offer solutions for core tasks that you have sparsely covered.

You may also want to look at devices or systems not directly competing with your device, but where you can find inspiration. If you design mobile phones, for example, it will be obvious to look at what core tasks are solved in the PC or tablet world. These core tasks may evolve into core tasks for mobile devices later.

If you are designing a word processor or some other piece of software, you will look for competition and try to dig out relevant core tasks from them. Or you will invite or ask lead users (as described in Chapter 13). But the key goal is to find un-solved target user needs and hence potential core tasks that apply to your product.

In the example with the music player for teenagers, you may have found poten-tial future core tasks already from the exercise described previously. Maybe you de-ducted some core tasks from latent end-user needs—for example, the task of play-ing games with friends on your device or sending text messages.

By looking at potential future core tasks you will have a unique opportunity to provide great user experience innovations. If you design your solutions very well, your company may even end up later being seen as the inventor of the specific solutions.

Potential future core tasks, however, have some inherent challenges also. Try to avoid focusing on solutions for these potential core tasks so much that you end up reducing the user experience of the already existing core tasks.

Step 5: Document Your Preliminary Core Tasks

You can now document the imagined and hence assumed core tasks that you have identified for the product you are designing. One way is to place each of the user needs in the center of a page and show the identified core tasks around it. Figure 5-7 shows this approach for a single user need from the music player example: "I love to hang out with my friends."

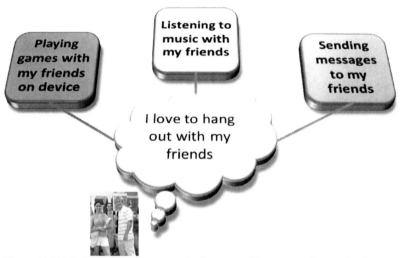

Figure 5-7. Method to show core tasks for a specific user need (music player example)

Step 6: Verify and Prioritize Your Core Tasks

Verifying your core tasks with target users is essential. Maybe you have misunderstood a user need. If the target users for the mobile phone you are designing have a need to protect their family, it may likely be a mistake to assume that you should build a full-blown camera surveillance system into your device. Maybe your users would never want to use your specific product to solve that need.

▧ **Note** If you invited users to your previous workshop, your core tasks may already be somewhat verified.

As another example, if you have a spreadsheet product, your product's users will likely also have needs to write documents. This does not, however, mean that you should integrate a word processor into your spreadsheet program, since the users may already have adequate means to solve this task.

Maybe you have overlooked an important user need, and this may also be revealed when verifying and prioritizing your core tasks with the users.

When verifying your core tasks, it is essential that you have the target users' prioritize the core tasks. And it is important that the target users have *your* type of product in mind for the prioritization. In this way, you will filter out core tasks that are relevant for the user, but for which there are sufficient solutions in other products (or that users would never see themselves performing on your type of device). For example, if you are designing a car key, and you have identified that writing text messages is a core task for your target users, you would hardly want to add that functionality to your key.

You can verify the core tasks by interviewing a number of target users face to face, or via phone or e-mail. You may also invite multiple target users into your office and let them prioritize in a team.

Make use of simple but effective methods to help users keep track of the big picture. For example, you can print each of your core tasks on separate pieces of paper and let the user arrange them in priority order, or place them in different categories, such as Very Important, Important, Less Important, and so on. Be sure to allow the users to discard core tasks and add new ones as well.

For the music player example, the result of the prioritization could be like that shown in Figure 5-8.

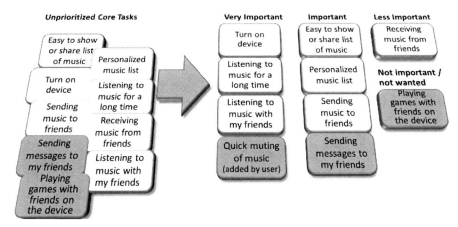

Figure 5-8. Prioritization of core tasks (music player example)

Step 7: Identify the Top Core Tasks for Your Product

If you are designing a new device, web page, or system, or you are designing a product for new target users, you will want to end up with a list of the most important core tasks. This is essential to ensure that the design of your product and your user experience innovations get focused.

If you instead already have a product that you need to find new user experience innovations for, you may want to focus your innovations on the most important core tasks, but you may also want to look at lower-priority core tasks for potential user experience innovation.

Step 8: Process and Document the Results

You now have a list of verified and prioritized core tasks for your product, and you may also have found a number of potential future core tasks. You can now document your core tasks in preparation for using them to drive innovation, as described in the next chapter. Consider including photos or drawings of each core task, together with some descriptive text. You can often find images of a specific situation from the Internet.

Summary

Identifying core tasks for your product will help you in identifying potential user experience innovations for a product that you are designing for new target users. Identifying core tasks is also essential for innovating user experience solutions for an existing product. Several of the following chapters will use core tasks—either directly or indirectly—as input into different methods for creating successful user experiences.

CHAPTER

Innovating Around Core Tasks

6

Many companies tend to spread their innovation across everything. You may stumble over web pages where seldom-used functions have been shined up radically, but where the basic navigation still lacks a lot. You may find devices (e.g., mobile phones) where small and irrelevant functions have been updated visually and user interactions have been improved, but where core functions (e.g., adding a contact to the contact list) still remain troublesome and old-fashioned. You may find web pages where the graphical experience has been improved radically, but where performing a task has not changed a bit.

These are examples of wrong focus on user experience innovation, and they show how focus is essential when creating successful user experience innovation. If you create a great innovation in a small and rarely used application of your product, then it will most likely not contribute to the overall success of your product.

The mistake in the previous situations is often that the core tasks of the product haven't been identified. Or they have been defined with, for example, a marketing or branding focus rather than a user focus.

The remainder of this chapter will describe a concrete approach to innovating potentially successful innovations that solve the core tasks in new ways. The approach consists of these six steps:

1. Identify target users, user needs, and core tasks.

2. Identify potential future core tasks.

3. List current solutions for the core tasks.

4. Evaluate the current solutions for the core tasks.

5. Innovate solutions.

6. Document the results and process the output.

Throughout the chapter, I will use a concrete example to explain the methods. In this chapter I have chosen to use a low-cost mobile phone, with a traditional keypad and a small black-and-white display. Figure 6-1 shows this phone.

Figure 6-1. Example used in this chapter: a low-cost mobile phone

Step 1: Identify Target Users, User Needs, and Core Tasks

In this chapter I will assume that you have already defined your target users, found their needs, and identified the core tasks, as described in the previous chapters. The target users for our example device are small business owners in low-income markets. Depending on the complexity of the product you have, there may be one, two, or many core tasks. In our specific example of a low-cost mobile device, the core tasks shown in Figure 6-2 have been identified.

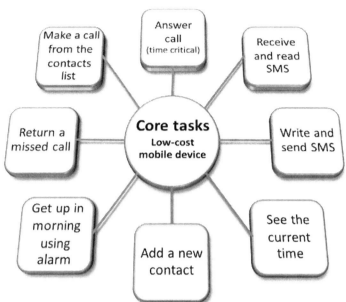

Figure 6-2. Example of core tasks for low-cost mobile device

Step 2: Identify Potential Future Core Tasks

Identifying future potential core tasks is extremely important. That knowledge helps you innovate new user experience solutions to cover latent or existing user needs. In the example with the low-cost mobile phone, let us assume that the company has identified the needs shown in Figure 6-3 that are currently not solved by the mobile device.

By looking at potential future core tasks you will have a unique opportunity to provide great user experience innovations. If you design your solutions very well, your company may even end up later being seen as the inventor of the specific solutions.

Potential future core tasks, however, have some inherent challenges also. For example, you might focus on solutions for potential core tasks so much that you end up reducing the user experience for the core tasks. To avoid this pitfall, you should try to treat existing core tasks and future core tasks equally when innovating.

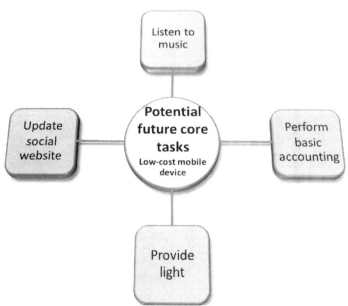

Figure 6-3. Potential future core tasks in the low-cost mobile device example

Step 3: List Current Solutions for the Core Tasks

When you have a complete list of core tasks for your device, system, or web page, you need to identify and evaluate the current solutions you offer for each. You can do this by creating a simple list with all the solutions that you already provide for each of the identified core tasks (e.g., on a whiteboard or similar).

Figure 6-4 shows the current solutions for a few of the core tasks identified for the low-cost mobile device.

You may have core tasks for which your product does not yet provide solutions. Retain those core tasks on the list. If you can find solutions for these core tasks, you might be able to easily create a successful innovation. For other core tasks, there may not yet be any suitable solutions available—but they may become feasible someday. Referring to your list of unsolved core tasks from time to time will keep you in a frame of mind to spot new possibilities as they arise.

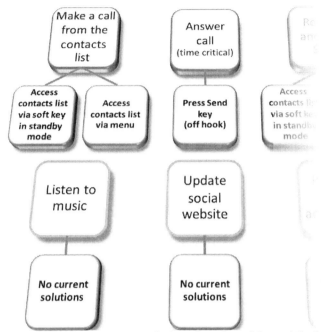

Figure 6-4. Listing current solutions for a few of the mobile device core tasks

Step 4: Evaluate the Current Solutions for the Core Tasks

When you have identified the current solutions for the core tasks, you then need to evaluate if the current solutions are adequate and sufficient. Even for core tasks where you have sufficient solutions, you will still want to create user experience innovations for these. You should never stop innovating around your core tasks, since you will want to constantly keep your solutions for the core tasks ahead of the competition.

There are several ways to evaluate your current solutions. You can run usability tests for the solutions to find pain points and areas needing improvement; you can have a user experience expert teardown made; and you can use market research and info from actual consumer feedback, via interviews or mail surveys.

Another way to evaluate the current solutions is to arrange a small meeting to discuss the current solutions specifically. You will again want a small but multidisciplinary group to do this. And you should invite consumer feedback experts as well as real users. Go through each of the core tasks and discuss how well the current solutions allow the users to solve these tasks.

You may want to start your user experience innovation for the core tasks where you find the most serious problems, and for the most important core tasks. But eventually you should go through all the core tasks.

Step 5: Innovate Solutions

No matter the current status of your solutions, the next step is to prepare each of the core tasks for innovation.

One method is reusing the list or drawing that you already created with the core tasks and their current solutions. You can quickly copy this drawing to a whiteboard, and you can then begin innovating. You can now invite a multidisciplinary team of innovative people to a session. As always, you may also want to invite real users—for example, a few lead users (as described further in Chapter 13).

The goal of the innovation session is to create new ideas or improvements to how the users can accomplish their core tasks. In the low-cost mobile phone example, let us assume that the creative session resulted in the new solutions shown in Figure 6-5.

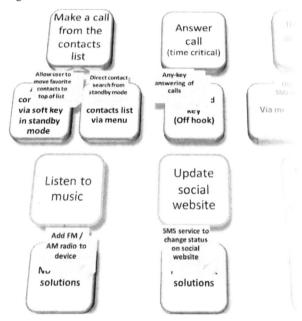

Figure 6-5. Examples of innovating solutions and improvements for core tasks

Step 6: Document the Results and Process the Output

How you choose to document the results and innovations is up to you. Figure 6-6 shows one example of how to document the results.

Eventually you'll want to start designing, creating drawings and wireframes, and so on, but first you need to verify your solutions with the users. You can, for example, verify solutions through usability tests and interviews.

You may also want to prioritize your solutions based on resources and time needed, but also on how crucial the core task is and on how often the user will need to perform this core task. You may, for example, want to give higher priority to improvements to core tasks that the user will perform every day or several times a day.

Also consider first impressions. If you are, for example, designing a website on which a core task is performed on the very front page, you should give high priority to improving this core task.

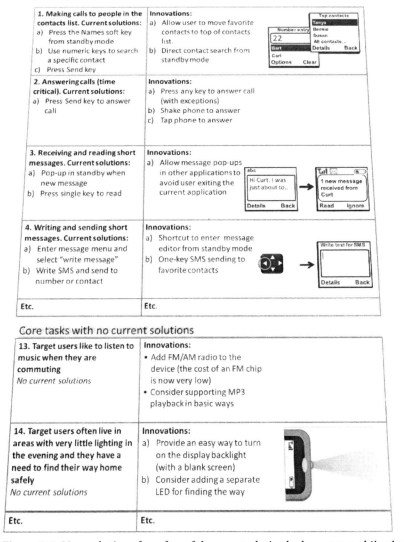

Figure 6-6. New solutions for a few of the core tasks in the low-cost mobile phone example

Summary

In this chapter I have shown you a concrete and straightforward way to create user experience innovations based on the core tasks of your device, web page, or system, and I have given you guidance on how to make these innovations successful.

CHAPTER

Innovating for New Technologies

7

Technologies themselves never, or at least very rarely, can make your product a success. To make your new technology a success, you have to provide value to the users from day one.

Anecdote

Infrared connection was available in early mobile phones, and it was mainly intended to connect your computer—via a very expensive and slow connection—to the Internet. Few cared, or were willing to pay, but the technology was there.

Nokia designed a two-player game named Snake (see Figure 7-1) using the infrared connection between two phones. That novel usage garnered much attention from the media. Many users tried and enjoyed the game. The logical conclusion is that new technologies will only become successful user experience innovations if and when the end users see a real value. In the case of Snake, the value was social entertainment, which at that time had never been seen on a mobile phone.

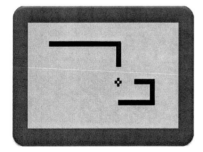

Figure 7-1. Two-player Snake, as seen on a Nokia phone

Selecting Technologies

Many technologies are added to devices, systems, or web pages for the wrong reasons. It can be because competitors use these technologies, it can be because the technology comes free with a chip-set's software package, or it can be because people in management decided to add the technology for some reason.

In my opinion, technologies should only be added or used if they can solve true end-user needs, be they needs for improved security, for greater interaction possibilities, or for any other user experience improvement.

If a specific technology does not improve the user experience or solve any existing or latent user needs, then adding the technology to your product will in the best case add extra costs to your product, and in the worst case degrade the user experience.

Technologies As Sources for User Experience Innovation

Technologies can, however, if added and designed in the correct way, be a truly great source for successful user experience innovation. Look at how multitouch display technology basically revolutionized the smart phone market. No, the technology itself did not revolutionize the smart phone market; the great and relevant user experience innovations created on top of this technology did.

In a similar way, the TV business went through a tremendous change during the 2000s due to the plasma, LCD, and LED technologies. This happened because the technologies were used to give clear benefits for the user experience: better-quality and larger-screened (yet lighter) TVs at a reasonable price.

For web pages, new HTML formats, Java capabilities, CSS support, and more can in similar ways be used to revolutionize the market, or at least your product. The key is to design with and use these features in ways that bring true value to the end user.

Keeping an eye on technologies and creating innovation around technologies is an absolute core method for successful user experience innovation. Many successful products in the world have taken existing or relatively new technologies and created a superb user experience around them.

Creating User Experience Innovation Around Technologies

One very practical and straightforward method to creating new ideas for a new (or old) technology is to draw the technology in the middle of a diagram (e.g., on a whiteboard), and then list potential or concrete customer needs around the technology. This method consists of five steps:

1. Identify target user needs.

2. Identify potential capabilities of the new technology.

3. Put the technology in the center.

4. Innovate solutions based on customer needs and technology capabilities.

5. Document the results and process the output.

Throughout this chapter I will use a specific example: a mobile device manufacturer that is planning to add an infrared camera to one of its devices. The main driver for the company is enabling users to take funny photos of people in dark rooms.

Step 1: Identify Target User Needs

The first thing you want to do as a designer and innovator is identify the needs of your target consumers. In the case of the infrared camera, your company has already defined family providers (Figure 7-2) in mature markets as the target users.

The core user needs are identified as these:

• The target users like to share photos with friends and family.

• Target users like to be creative.

• Security and safety is important for the target users—for themselves and their families.

• Target users like to have fun and play games, maybe with their families.

• Price and economy is important for the target users.

• Health is important.

You can diagram these needs, and their related potentials, as shown in Figure 7-3. I use the term *potentials* to refer to specific uses to which users can put a device that meets the listed needs. For example, health needs suggest the potential for using the infrared camera to look for medical symptoms, perhaps to measure body temperature.

How you choose to document the core needs is up to you, but I suggest using a whiteboard, since later you may want to invite more people to brainstorm ideas based on your initial framework. But if you prefer mind-mapping software or other media, this may also work fine. Just make sure that the tool does not become an obstacle to the actual innovation process. Innovating in a team around a single computer is often not optimal.

Figure 7-2. Family provider

Figure 7-3. User needs in the infrared camera example

Step 2: Identify Potential Capabilities of the New Technology

The next thing you may want to do is to search the Internet or literature to find out what your technology can be used for. List both the obvious and not-so-obvious potential capabilities.

Sometimes a technology—with a small twist—can be changed to be used for completely different purposes than intended, and this can expand the use cases for the technology. And it may give you an idea that can give you a successful user experience innovation.

In the case of the device with an infrared camera, you may find out that such cameras have the potential capabilities shown in Figure 7-4.

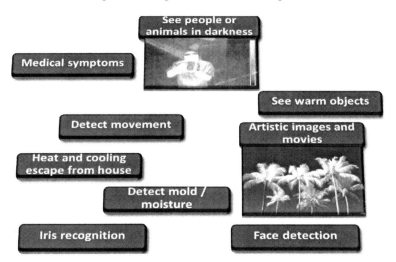

Figure 7-4. Technology capabilities of the infrared camera

Not all of these capabilities may feel directly relevant in the beginning, but try to make a complete list nevertheless. Sometimes looking at a technology and its potentials from a completely different angle may bring up truly new and potentially successful innovations for your specific product.

You can then list the potential capabilities of your technology as shown in Figure 7-5.

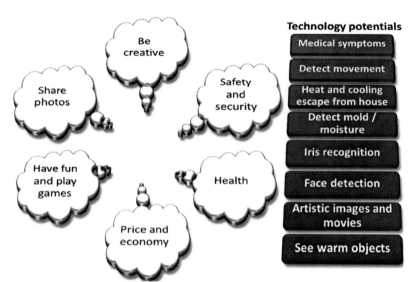

Figure 7-5. *Potential capabilities listed next to the needs of the target consumer*

Step 3: Put the Technology in the Center

The next thing you want to do is to place your technology in the center of the diagram. You are then basically ready to start innovating potentially successful user experience innovation.

In the case of the infrared camera, your drawing may now look like that shown in Figure 7-6.

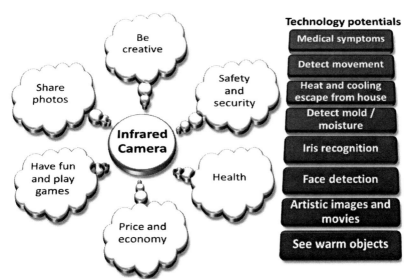

Figure 7-6. Innovating around a central technology

Step 4: Innovate Solutions Based on Customer Needs and Technology Capabilities

You are now basically ready to start your idea creation for your technology. As with all creativity, more brains work better, and people from different disciplines may come up with very different ideas. So make sure to invite enough—but not too many—people to your idea creation session. You may even want to invite real users, as described in Chapter 13. Using a large whiteboard is usually best, and it allows multiple participants to write on the board at the same time. You may also use sticky notes, allowing users who don't like to stand in front of a whiteboard to sit at their desk and write down ideas to be put on the whiteboard.

Creative sessions should not have too many rules or limitations, so choose the method that fits your team and situation best, and allow for ongoing changes to the method. You may also need to add new technology capabilities if some participants are aware of other potential uses of your technology. However, the goal is to focus on the connections between your technology and the target user needs. In other words, the focus is on connections in the figure. Also, new needs may be added during the process, if participants are aware of target customer needs that you overlooked when planning your creative session.

The connections between user needs and the technology will be the key focus of the idea creation. In the case of the infrared camera, the result could look like Figure 7-7 after just a few minutes of idea creation.

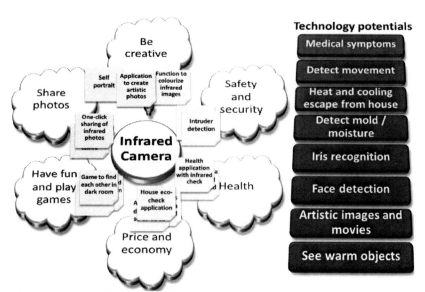

Figure 7-7. Example of result of innovation around the infrared camera

Step 5: Document the Results and Process the Output

The results of your efforts will be a huge list of big and small ideas. You can choose to merge or split ideas, or massage them further—as a part of the innovation session or afterward. You can also verify those results, as described later in Chapter 18.

Your ideas will most likely fit the customer needs quite well, since this method is based around the target users' core needs; but you should of course verify the ideas later on with customers. You can verify solutions through market research, through simple interviews where you present your ideas to potential target customers, and later through usability testing and other common methods.

In the case of adding an infrared camera to a device, the resulting list from your creative session may be something like that shown Figure 7-8. You will want to keep the end-user needs as the headings for the resulting ideas list, since it is very important to remember—especially later in the design and verification process—why these ideas came up and why they might bring value to your customers. There will also be ideas that do not cover an identified end-user need. These should also be documented. You may be able to twist them to apply to an end-user need, or fit them into a future product designed for a different target group.

Share photos:	Being creative:	Safety and security:
• One-click sharing of infrared photos by uploading them to a predefined web server. • Automatically sharing of all infrared photos to community. • Allow tagging of photos easily to allow others to see what the object of your infrared photo is.	• Specific application to create and edit artistic photos. • Specific application to create artistic, fun, or scary infrared self-portraits. • Provide options for photo capturing, autocoloring, different modes, etc. • Downloadable profiles and modes for your infrared camera, allowing different effects when taking photos.	• Provide charging stand where the device can stand so that the infrared camera can detect intruders. • Intruder application where camera will detect intruders and start alarm or send text message to a mobile phone. • Find your way in darkness. A special application to be used to find your way in darkness.
Have fun and play games:	**Price and economy:**	**Health:**
• Game where several players can try to find and catch other users in a dark room or outside at night time. The game may also use other technologies (e.g., Bluetooth) to detect proximity of other people. • A family game for exploring nature (e.g., for detecting small animals at night).	• Using infrared camera (and maybe other technologies) to see where heating or cooling is escaping from your house. • Eco-Check application with questions and answers on how to save money on heating and cooling.	• Guided health application that monitors health by taking infrared images of the body and also asking questions of the user.. • Mold detection application. A special mode for the infrared camera to detect mold in old or flooded houses.

Ideas not fitting any target user needs:
- Programmable remote control transmitter for your TV
- Animal surveillance. Send an SMS when an animal enters or leaves the house, using infrared camera to detect movement and to detect what kind of animal.
- Autotagging normal (and infrared) photos by automatically identifying the persons you are taking photo of. Using infrared camera to identify who the persons are.
- Game hunting

Figure 7-8. Resulting idea list for a device with an infrared camera

Using Core Tasks or Pain Points as an Alternative Approach

In this chapter I chose to use the target users for the user experience innovation, but you may also try this same exercise using core tasks or pain points around the technology. You may get a few other ideas when approaching this exercise in other ways.

Summary

When adding a new technology to a device, web page, or system, many companies tend to focus on the already known and planned use cases for that application. If the competition already has products on the market covering the core uses of the technology, then you will have little chance of making a real difference to the users—or in the market.

The method described in this chapter ensures two things:

- It ensures that you will have already found and studied other potential uses of the technology that is being applied to a product

- It ensures that the customers' needs are the focal point of your innovation process, hence making it much more probable that your solutions will actually give value to the end users.

The next chapter will give ideas on how to create user experience innovation aroundapplications, applications.

Innovating for Applications

8

When adding a new application to your web page, device, or system, you will often focus primarily on the core use cases of this application. If you, for example, add a calendar to a web page or a device, you will usually focus mainly on the presentation, on creating easy methods to add reminders, on alarm handling, and so on.

However, there is huge potential if you also start looking at how your new application can *interact* with other applications and parts of your product. Looking at these interactions can help you find user experience innovations in the links between applications.

By innovating in the links between applications, you can provide users a seamless experience, and this can truly distinguish your product in the market. Many brilliant web pages, devices, and systems are unique not because of the actual design of the standalone applications they have, but because of the seamless integration of multiple applications, which gives the entire product or set of products a great and powerful user experience.

In this chapter I describe a five-step process that I have used many times with success. The process helps you examine links between applications with the goal of providing a seamless and delightful user experience. The five steps for this method are as follows:

1. Identify target user needs.
2. Identify applications to interact with.
3. Create a diagram with your application in the center.
4. Innovate solutions.
5. Document the results and process the output.

In this chapter I will again use a concrete example to describe the method. We will consider a social community web page. Our scenario will be that we want to add an events calendar to that web page.

Step 1: Identify Target User Needs

The first thing you want to do is identify the target user needs for your web page, device, or system. You can do that based on market research, interviews with users, hotline feedback, and so on. For our example involving a calendar for a social web page, the target user needs shown in Figure 8-1 were identified.

Target user needs

Remember birthday of friends and family

Meet with friends

Share photos

Share information & status with friends

Dating

Partying

Figure 8-1. Target user needs identified for the social community web page example

Step 2: Identify Applications to Interact With

The first thing to do is identify any potential applications that the new application could interact with. If you're designing for a web page or mobile device, you might want to include applications, technologies, and services from other web pages or mobile devices as well.

Again, I suggest using a whiteboard for the method I describe in this chapter. Write down your target user needs from Figure 8-1. Then build a circle of applications that the web page already offers, as in Figure 8-2.

In this example, I'm assuming that the web page already supports a friends list, photo sharing, status messages, and message handling. I've also placed "Other web services" in the diagram.

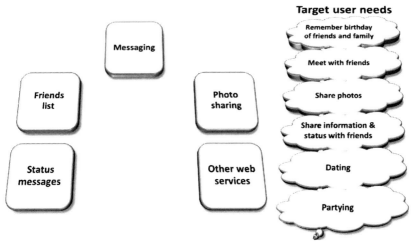

Figure 8-2. Placing other applications in a circle

Step 3: Create a diagram with your application in the center

The next step is to put the application you want to innovate around in the center, and connect it to the other applications available on your device, web page, or system. In this example, we will put the calendar in the center, as shown in Figure 8-3.

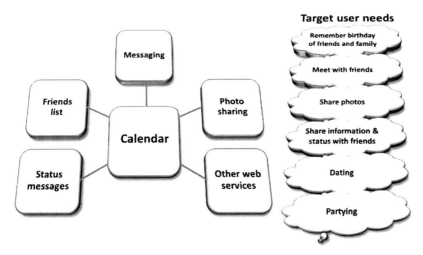

Figure 8-3. Calendar placed in the middle and connected to the existing applications

Step 4: Innovate Solutions

You are now ready to gather a group of people to start your user experience innovation process. You should focus your innovation effort on connections between your new application in the center and the other applications. It is in those in-between areas that you will find truly novel and potentially successful user experience innovations. But the target user needs are equally important and can be used as inspiration in the idea creation process.

During your innovation process, ideas will surely pop up that relate only to the application that you have in focus. You will also likely generate ideas for the other applications. It is important to also focus on how the applications may interact with others not in the diagram—in our case with other web services outside of our social community website. For this example, the result of the idea creation session could look like that shown in Figure 8-4.

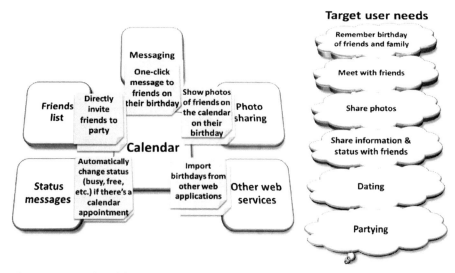

Figure 8-4. *Results of the innovation for the calendar application*

Step 5: Document the Results and Process the Output

You will be surprised at how many ideas you can generate in a very short time using this method. The resulting list of ideas of course needs further verification with customers, marketing, and so forth. You may also need to create draft design sketches for the ideas before verifying the ideas with your users.

A filtered version of the resulting list may look like Figure 8-5.

Calendar – Friends List:
- Application to easily drag and drop friends from the friends list to an arrangement or party on the calendar.
- Show birthdays for friends directly in the friends list as well as on the calendar.
- Create a dating entry on the calendar. This will be visible to all and can be accepted by others.
- Allow sharing parts or all of your calendar with friends.

Calendar – Messaging:
- Offer a one-click shortcut to send a message from calendar to friends having birthday.
- Allow from messaging to send calendar reminders to friends.
- Allow from calendar to send arrangements as a text message to friends etc.
- Allow user to store reminders, which will make a message be sent automatically on a specific date (for example on a person's birthday).

Calendar – Photo Sharing:
- Show photos of friends on the calendar when they have a birthday or when you have arrangements booked with them
- Define a date for when certain photos will be shared, or when the sharing of the photos will end.
- Use calendar to specify date taken for photos.

Calendar – Status Messages:
- Automatic update of status message if the user is busy, at a party, or similar.
- Change user's status message automatically on his or her birthday.

Calendar – Other Web Services:
- Import birthdays from social media sites.
- Automatically show weather forecast for the next coming days in the calendar.
- Show events on the calendar based on the user's interests and location/home address (e.g., show events such as parties, exhibitions, movie theater info, etc.).

Figure 8-5. Results of innovation for the calendar example

Summary

The method described in this chapter provides a tangible approach to creating user experience innovation for and around a specific application. The method works by focusing on how the application can become more powerful and valuable by closely integrating its functionality with other applications already existing on your device, web page, or system.

Another important part of successful user experience innovation around applications is looking at the ecosystem. I talk more about ecosystems and how to examine them in Chapter 12.

The focus on target customer needs in this chapter ensures a good chance of success at innovating in the spaces between applications, and as such a good chance of success in the marketplace. The method has proven successful for generating a large number of ideas relevant to the user, many of which you will find on Nokia's mobile devices today.

CHAPTER

Relieving the Pain

9

It is surprising how many device manufacturers and professional website companies have little or no idea of their products' pain points for the users. Every day I stumble upon web pages that take tens of seconds or even minutes to simply load the Flash intro; and very often those web pages do not even have a skip-intro function available. In those cases, I do like 90 percent of other users: I leave the web page. According to Jakob Nielsen,[1] a 10-second delay in web page loading may often make users leave the site.

I frequently unsuccessfully look for essential information on a web page. For example, I might look for details about a company's products. Instead I am presented with useless information about the company's history or how its stocks are doing.

Currently spending most of my time in many different hotel rooms, I also repeatedly find myself trying to figure out how to operate the TV with the remote control. Usually the problem is that remote controls are plastered with buttons, leaving the core functions almost impossible to find. The layout of the keys certainly also leaves a lot to wish for.

As mentioned earlier in this book, it may take ten great user experience elements to cover up for a single bad user experience element in a product. And if your bad user experience is placed where most users tend to navigate, then you have a serious problem.

Benefits

Focusing your innovation on experiences that are painful for the user is a good investment and will enhance the overall user experience of your product. Fixing the pain points will not only improve end-user satisfaction, but it will almost certainly also save you a lot of money that would have been spent replying to e-mails and taking calls on hotlines. Fixing pain points may not necessarily give you a product with a superb user experience, but it will help you avoid having a product with a very bad user experience.

My experience is that *finding* the pain points is often not a problem; however, rigid organizations, stubbornness in the design department, management, and marketing often force these problems to go unfixed. Sometimes problematic software architectures and lack of resources tend to be a problem, since fixing a pain

---

[1] Jacob Nielsen's Alertbox, June 21, 2010, Website Response Times
http://www.useit.com/alertbox/response-times.html

point may take the same amount of time as designing new functionality that the marketing department is requesting. Fixing a pain point will typically be prioritized below designing new functionality, but in many cases this will be a very bad way to prioritize.

Anecdote

Sometimes fixing pain points may even generate new ideas that can become selling points for your product. In the early days of mobile communication, most phones were equipped with very simple contact lists. Although these lists supported names, the handling of them was very cumbersome.

One of the most successful early mobile phones was the Nokia 2110 (shown in Figure 9-1). It had a contact list where the user could add a name for phone numbers. Accessing the list was relatively easy, via a soft key labeled "Memory," which could be accessed from standby mode. However, when pressing this soft key, you would be presented with a list of numbers organized according to their more or less random locations on the SIM card. The names of the contacts were not even visible.

To allow switching from SIM card–order mode to an alphabetical list of names, the 2110 was equipped with a dedicated key labeled "abc" (the top right button above the keypad in Figure 9-1). Most users would have to read the manual to understand what this key did, and few users actually read it. Since research and interviews showed that very few users were actually using the alphabetic contact list, the conclusion for many people in marketing was that users didn't actually want an alphabetical contact list—an incorrect assumption.

Luckily, the misguided people in marketing did not get their say. Keen and proactive user experience designers at Nokia managed to push through a radically new and later very successful redesign of the contacts list. This new design also made the abc key superfluous, which—due to the sparse real estate on the device—may have contributed to why the new contact list design was approved.

Figure 9-1. The Nokia 2110 . Copyright Nokia 2011

The Method

The method described in this chapter is a straightforward and simple way to find the pain points in your product's user experience and to create innovations that reduce those pain points. The five steps in this method are

1. Identify the current pain points of your product.

2. Find the underlying causes for the pain points.

3. Verify your causes.

4. Innovate solutions.

5. Document the results and process the output.

Throughout the description of the steps, I will use a concrete example. In this case, the example will be the remote control for a TV. I'll assume that the remote control currently looks like that shown in Figure 9-2. I have deliberately under-designed the remote control, and of course avoided referring to any existing branded models. Many of the functions, however, may well resemble those of the remote control you have in your living room.

Figure 9-2. TV remote control used as example

Step 1: Identify Current Pain Points

When thinking about the number of devices, web pages, and systems that are basically spammed with serious pain points, you can imagine that identifying these pain points might be very difficult. However, nothing could be more wrong. Pain points are some of the easiest things to find in your product.

The problem in many organizations is that fixing pain points is seldom given high priority. Nevertheless, you will need to start by identifying the pain points in your product. Following are some of my own favorite methods, because they are simple, easy, and cheap—and they work.

Hotlines and Mail Feedback

Simply ask the people dealing with customer feedback about what questions they tend to get asked most. Alternatively, skim through some of the many files that they have with feedback, ideas, and complaints. It may take a day or two to do this work, but the results may well be worth it.

Use the Internet

You may easily find complaints about your product on the Web. Some users will start to dislike your product a lot if there are too many pain points, and in their anger they will post blog entries or even launch entire websites dedicated to complaining about your product. Search out those blog entries and sites. Don't view those people as a menace. Instead, use the valuable information they offer about what they dislike.

Usability Tests

Usability tests—on a small or large scale—often reveal many pain points. A typical mistake is to only document and fix the problems found in new applications or features that you've just designed and tested. Also consider pain points found in your existing applications, features, and products.

User Interviews

Simply find a few of your current end users, and interview them about pain points. People may sometimes be too polite, so make sure that you really get them to open up about the problems they experience with your product.

User Experience Expert Teardown

A *teardown* is when you specifically assign someone the task of tearing apart your design and looking for problems. This is sometimes the easiest, simplest, and cheapest method for finding pain points. Hire a good user experience expert for a few hours to review your web page, device, or system, and you will be amazed by how many pain points he can produce. As mentioned, finding pain points is not difficult, and with the mindset that a good user experience expert has, it is a simple and fast task. However, as a rule of thumb, never use the designer who designed the application being examined. The reasons are obvious—try to find somebody else.

Pain Points in a TV Remote Control

In our TV remote example, the company has identified the pain points shown in Figure 9-3. In this case, the company used a user experience expert (me) to find the pain points—in less than half an hour. I am sure that you'll recognize many of these pain points, since they exist on a majority of TV remote controls.

Figure 9-3. *Pain points in the TV remote control example*
Source of photo: nuchylee, FreeDigitalPhotos.net (www.freedigitalphotos.net)

Step 2: Find the Underlying Causes

Pain points often do not tell you what the actual problem is, and they rarely tell you how to solve the problem. Before actually creating solutions for the pain pointsyour task is to try to find out what the underlying reasons for the pain points are. For this, you may again use different approaches. You will probably need a small group of people from different disciplines to come together and examine the causes.

You can, for example, invite a small group of people for a session. You may want to invite people from marketing, interaction design, industrial design, user experience, mechanics, consumer feedback, and so on. Who you need to invite will depend on the nature of your product (device, system, web page, software system, etc.), and it will depend on the size and organizational setup of your company. The group does not need to be larger than four to eight people, and the time you want to spend doing this does not have to be more than one or two hours.

You may also want to invite real users. You might want to contact the person behind one of the websites disliking your product, and invite the person to the session, paying for his or her flight and hotel for one or two days. You will not only get very valuable feedback from this person, but you might also change his or her mind about your product and company.

The method you want to use with the group that you assemble is to start imagining what could be the causes of the problems that the users are experiencing. Go through each pain point one by one. You will be surprised at how easy it is to do that, and how many potential causes you can come up with in a very short time.

Figure 9-4 shows an example from the process of finding causes of pain points in the remote control example. In the sections to follow, I will go through potential causes for all the pain points in the TV remote control example. I'll be looking at the very same pain points illustrated in Figure 9-3.

Figure 9-4. Identifying causes for a specific pain point
Source of photo: nuchylee, FreeDigitalPhotos.net (www.freedigitalphotos.net)

The Remote Control Does Not Work Unless I Point It Directly at the TV

You may have equipped your remote control with an infrared diode that is simply too weak. Maybe you continued to use the same cheap diode that you used when TVs were rarely larger than 30 inches in size and when people never sat more than 10 feet away from the TV when watching and controlling it.

Maybe you designed the front of your remote control wrong. Maybe the industrial designer wanted a smooth front on the remote control, and maybe that decision meant a compromise in which the infrared diode had to sink deeper into the product, hence reducing the user experience radically.

Maybe the batteries are used up too fast, or maybe the user does not know when the batteries are low and should be replaced. These are all potential causes to examine. The point during brainstorming is not necessarily to eliminate causes, but rather to list those possible causes deserving a closer look.

Many Times, the Remote Control Seems to Not Be Working, but Then I Realize It's Pointing in the Wrong Direction

Holding the control in the wrong orientation is a classic and widespread problem with remote controls. Many remote controls are designed in a way that makes it almost impossible to *feel* whether they are being held in the correct orientation.

Designers tend to forget the conditions under which most of their target users will need to operate the TV and hence the remote control. The target users will primarily use the TV in the evening, when it is often dark. The users will tend in many cases to try to reduce the light in the room to enjoy the TV or movie experience in an optimal way. In short, a TV remote control is very often operated in darkness.

So the cause of this problem of poor orientation is most often an inadequate design of the remote control. There is no easy way to feel from the shape or the weight distribution of the remote control what is up and down. The few keys that the user can distinguish by running their fingers over the remote control are placed in the middle, leaving no chance for the user to use these keys as guidance. The two ends of the remote control have similarly shaped keys, also leaving no way for a hand or fingers to distinguish the front from the back.

The Remote Control No Longer Works; I Keep Changing the Batteries, but After a Few Weeks It Stops Working Again

Failure of a remote to control the device *can* be caused by bad hardware design that drains the batteries too quickly. However, in my experience, this problem is most often caused by *mode keys*, such as in Figure 9-5. Some creative designer or clever consumer insight "expert" may have figured out that customers do not like having many remote controls to control the different devices in their living room. This resulted in the creation of mode keys, which a user must remember to press first to choose which possible target device to control.

Figure 9-5. Mode keys

The need to reduce remote control clutter may actually be a true and valid user need to solve (this is complicated by the fact that many people own TV, VCR, and DVD players from different manufacturers). So users may indeed have a true need to control multiple devices with a single remote control. But that is not why the problem described in this section occurs. The problem occurs due to a badly designed solution for how to operate multiple devices.

Users can accidentally press one of the mode keys quite easily. This can happen when they try to operate the device when it points in the wrong direction, or when they accidentally sit on the remote control if it's lying on the sofa. If they, for example, change to DVD mode, the remote control will simply stop working, and the users will be unable to change channels, change the volume, or even switch the TV on or off.

Some manufactures have invented a (pretty bad) solution to the problem. With some devices, if you remove the batteries, the mode will return to TV mode. In such cases, users will then experience that replacing the batteries will solve the problem. (On the other hand, remote controls from some other manufacturers will remember the last mode even after the batteries are changed).

Mode buttons are a brilliant example of a design that tries to solve the user needs of a limited amount of users (those who own the same brand for all their TV devices and those who also understand the concept of the mode keys). However, combined with poor design, mode keys can turn the overall user experience into a very bad one. This is exactly the way to get customers to really dislike your product.

I Only Use the Volume Keys and the Zapper Keys, but It Is a Real Hassle to Find These Keys in a Dark Room

This time the user states that she has problems operating the remote in a dark room. And the user also states what functions are core for her: changing channels and adjusting volume. Of course, a single statement like this may not truly represent which keys average users use most often, but it does give a hint. And this hint can be used to dig further into the usage of different keys.

I do not have any precise statistical data, but I would guess that these four keys (volume up/down and channel up/down) would account for more than 90 percent of all key presses on any TV remote control. A company producing TVs and remote controls would probably have some data on this, or they could find out by simply looking at the wear and tear on the different keys when remote controls are returned for repair.

Almost no TV remote controls take this typical and limited use of the remote control into account. Figure 9-6 shows one design in common use, but the keys are difficult to find in the dark. Figure 9-7 shows another design, one commonly found in hotel rooms. The circular pattern is easy enough to find, but many hotel room remotes actually use other keys for volume control, leaving the keys in the circle for less important tasks.

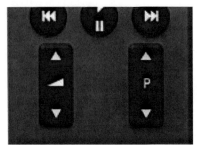

Figure 9-6. These keys are needed often but are hard to find in darkness.

Figure 9-7. These keys are easy to find in darkness, but they cannot be used for volume and zapping.

I Cannot Turn the Volume Down Quickly Enough When I Have to Answer a Phone Call

This is a very precisely described pain point. But finding the cause of this is slightly trickier. Here are some possibilities to consider:

- Maybe the volume keys work too slowly.

- Maybe it comes back to the problem that the user needs to point the remote control directly at the TV for it to work (which is tricky when you're also reaching for your ringing phone).

- Maybe the mute key is too hidden or difficult to find in darkness.

- Maybe the wording or icon for your mute button is not understood by many users.

The pain point does indicate that the user is not aware of the mute key, since the user specifically explains that turning down the volume is too slow. This should put some extra focus on making the mute button easy to understand and find— even in a dark room.

My Remote Control Stopped Working Because I Repeatedly Dropped It on the Floor; I Had to Buy a New and Very Expensive Replacement

This is a case where you really need to dig a bit deeper to find the cause. Maybe your customer is just very clumsy, but if you have several customers with the same problem, you may need to look for other causes.

It could be that the weight distribution of the remote control is bad. Maybe it is too heavy on one end. Figure 9-8 shows such a remote—one that might be easily dropped while operating the lower keys.

Figure 9-8. The user could easily drop the remote when operating the lower keys.

Maybe the user often picks up the remote from the wrong end since the remote control does not allow the fingers or hand to feel which way is correct. Or maybe the most-used keys are placed in an ergonomically poor position.

Anecdote

My experience in the mobile phone industry is that a very large percentage of mobile devices need repair due to exposure to water. This water can often be traced back to a toilet. The owners of such devices are in most cases male.

The upfront reason is obvious. Men write a lot of messages while standing over the toilet. However, the true cause is slightly trickier and involves the location of certain buttons on the devices and how those buttons are used when writing text messages.

I must admit to being one of the original designers of the function of the star key (*)for texting. The star key allows one to easily get the next match when using predictive text input. The key's location combined with the typical weight of a mobile device makes it very easy for users (at least right-handed ones) to accidentally drop the phone when pressing that key (see Figure 9-9).

History will teach you. When I designed this little shortcut for text writing, SMS was hardly used by anyone. And I certainly never imagined that so much texting would be done over a toilet.

Figure 9-9. A common way to flood a mobile phone

Step 3: Verify Your Causes

After identifying potential causes for your pain points, you are now ready to verify these causes. This step is important, since you cannot be sure if your causes are correct. Maybe people will drop your remote control purely due to poor weight distribution of your device, and hence you will not need to use resources on redesigning the keypad layout.

Why change the entire physical design of your device if the problem is purely in the weight distribution? Why redesign an entire application if people only have problems with the wording of one specific function? Fixing nonexistent problems is of course a waste of time, and you may even introduce new pain points or other problems when doing this.

There may be several approaches to verifying your causes, but it is difficult to do without consulting the people who originally stated the pain points. So you will need to approach the users—or at least the user experience experts—that provided you with the pain points.

Simple phone interviews with users may do the trick. Short e-mails asking about the different causes may be another approach. Inviting the users that had pain points for a face-to-face session is a third.

You will need to describe the different causes that you came up with for their pain points, and you can ask the users what they believe is the true cause. Several causes may be true for the same pain point, so also allow the users to give more than one cause. Finally, the users may state that none of the proposed causes are true. In this case you will need to ask further questions of the user to try to find the real causes.

In the TV remote control example, we will assume that the verified causes identified for each of the pain points are as listed in Figure 9-10.

The remote control is not working unless I point it directly at the TV. It is so annoying • The LED used is simply not strong enough.	Many times, the remote control is not working, but then I realise that is turns in the wrong direction • There is no way for the user to feel in a dark room how the right direction of the remote control is.	The remote control does no longer work. I keep changing the batteries, but after a few weeks it stops working again • The user has accidentally pressed a mode key
I only use the volume keys and the zapper keys. But it is a real hassle to find these keys in a dark room • The keypad layout does not allow the user to easily find the most frequently used keys. • The design of the remote control does not make it easy for the user to point the remote control in the right direction.	I cannot turn volume down quick enough if my telephone is ringing • The mute button was understood and found by the user. • The mute button is placed in an awkward and illogical location • The remote control is very sensitive to the direction	My remote control stopped working because I repeatedly dropped it on the floor. I had to buy a new and very expensive replacement • The user often picks up the remote control facing the wrong way • Essential and frequently used keys are placed in a location which makes it very easy to drop the remote control.

Figure 9-10. Verified causes for the pain points in the remote control example

Step 4: Innovate Solutions

When you know the actual causes of your pain points, you are ready to start innovating solutions to solve your pain points. The verified causes are similar to any other design input: you have a specific problem that needs to be solved. As always, more brains work better than one, so invite people from various disciplines in your organization, and also consider inviting lead users, as described in Chapter 13.

One approach is illustrated in Figure 9-11 using the TV remote control example. The figure shows a single pain point placed in the center, and the verified causes for the pain point placed around it. Ideas can then be added with sticky notes or similar.

Some causes may be hard to tackle, but this is where true creativity comes in handy. Let me give an example. You have realized a serious pain point on your website when users try to load a photo album. The cause is that it simply takes time to load large images from the user's computer.

In this case you need to be creative. Increasing the basic Internet speed for your customers is of course not an option. But there are many other ways to speed up the loading of images, or at least to give the effect of speeding things up. The solutions would fall into two categories:

1. *Technical solutions*: You may choose to use smaller versions of a user's photos when loading the photo album (e.g., lower-resolution photos, different image formats, etc.).

2. *User experience solutions*: A typical user experience solution in this case would be to make it *look* like the loading of the photos goes faster than it actually does. This can be achieved by giving instant feedback to the user when opening the photo album (the worst type of waiting is when nothing happens). You may also choose to start by loading very rough and hence small versions of the user's photos, which are then replaced with the higher-quality versions.

   Or you may try to make the waiting time more pleasurable. Adding pleasure to the waiting time can be done by providing constant visual feedback to the user about the progress, or maybe adding a very simple game during the waiting time (popping balloons on the screen or similar). Just be sure that these additions don't slow down the process even more.

As you see from this example, finding solutions to pain points is not that difficult when you know the underlying causes of the pain points.

Figure 9-11 shows an example of innovating solutions for causes of TV remote control pain points. To complete the remote control example, the subsequent sections will list a number of potential solutions for all the verified causes of the pain points.

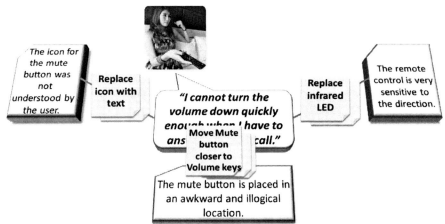

Figure 9-11. Example of innovating for a specific pain point with known causes.
Source of photo: nuchylee, FreeDigitalPhotos.net (www.freedigitalphotos.net)

The Remote Control Does Not Work Unless I Point It Directly at the TV

The cause is that the LED used is simply not strong enough. The following are possible solutions:

- Replace the LED with a stronger one.

- Use a magnifying lens—or a lens that spreads the infrared light—in front of the LED.

Many Times, the Remote Control Seems to Not Be Working, but Then I Realize It's Pointing in the Wrong Direction

The cause is that there is no way for the user to feel in a dark room what the right orientation of the remote control is. In this case, a number of solutions could be valid, such as the following:

- Change the weight distribution (e.g., make the bottom heavier by moving the batteries to this area). This will also make operation of keys located low on the device easier, because the weight will still be resting in the user's hand.

- Move keys that are easily distinguishable by fingers from the middle of the device to one of the ends. The user will over time learn this and hence know how to turn the remote control correctly. Figure 9-12 shows one possible approach.

Figure 9-12. Often-used and easily distinguishable buttons moved to one end

- Leave an area without keys at the lower part of the remote control. This will not only make the orientation easy to distinguish with the fingers, but it may also improve operation of the lower keys on the keypad. Figure 9-12 shows this approach as well.

- Create a different form factor with a clearly distinguishable top and bottom (see the final solution later, in Figure 9-15).

- Add a non-disturbing LED light to your remote control indicating the correct orientation of the device (see the final solution in Figure 9-15 for an example of this approach).

The Remote Control No Longer Works; I Keep Changing the Batteries, but After a Few Weeks It Stops Working Again

The cause is that the user has accidentally pressed a mode key. There may be several solutions to this problem. Several of the following solutions can be combined to attack this problem:

- Simply remove the mode feature. It is not a shame to realize that you have created a design for a small minority of users that has ended up as a pain point for a majority of users. Leaving a serious pain point and a reason for frustration is worse.

- Move all operation of other devices to a simple and effective onscreen menu.

- Design the mode keys to be flatter and almost impossible to press by accident.

- Use an LED to light up the mode key related to the currently selected mode every time a key is pressed (I have seen this concept used on even very cheap programmable remote controls). This may (or may not) indicate to the user that the mode has been changed.

- Keep the mode buttons but allow them to affect only two to four functions typically needed to operate each of the other devices. The mode keys could then naturally be placed above and together with the function keys affected by the mode change, as shown in Figure 9-13.

Figure 9-13. Redesigned mode concept

I Only Use the Volume Keys and the Zapper Keys, but It Is a Real Hassle to Find These Keys in a Dark Room

One cause is that the keypad layout does not allow the user to easily find the most frequently used keys. The solutions for this cause could be as follows:

- Allow the easily distinguishable five-way key to work as channel up/down key as well as a volume control key, as many older remote controls do. For many new remote controls, these prominent and easy-to-find keys only work inside menus.

- Position the five-way control at a more prominent location on the remote control (see Figure 9-12, in the previous section).

- Remove keys that have functions that are used very rarely. Place the functions in menus or similar instead.

Another cause is that the design of the remote control does not make it easy for the user to point the remote control in the right direction. The solutions here are the same as those in the earlier section on orientation. You can reshape the remote or change the weight distribution, or do other things to make it easy for users to orient the device sight-unseen.

I Cannot Turn the Volume Down Quickly Enough When I Have to Answer a Phone Call

One cause is that the mute button was not identified or understood by the user. This issue can be solved by changing the icon of the mute button, by replacing the icon, or by adding text to the button. Adding text is not always the best solution, since it is language dependent, and most TV manufacturers do not want to create a specific remote control for every language in the world. However, replacing the icon with a better one and combining it with a text label may help the situation.

Another cause is that the mute button is placed in an awkward and illogical location. This can be solved by moving the mute button closer to the volume control buttons. The four-way scroll keys are already used for controlling volume, and so is the mute button, so why not place these buttons close to each other? One idea could be to place the mute key in the center of the four-way key, as shown in Figure 9-14. Another idea could be to place the mute button right below the volume keys to indicate that pressing this button will turn the volume all the way down.

Figure 9-14. Mute button relabeled and placed close to the volume control keys

A third cause could be that the remote control is very sensitive to direction. This has already been covered. Choose one or more of the solutions to help users identify and maintain proper orientation, and implement those solutions.

My Remote Control Stopped Working Because I Repeatedly Dropped It on the Floor; I Had to Buy a New and Very Expensive Replacement

One cause is that the user often picks up the remote control facing the wrong way. Several of the previously suggested solutions may solve this problem, but it could also be beneficial to change the design of the remote control to have a good grip.

Another cause is that essential and frequently used keys are placed in a location that makes it very easy to drop the remote control. The solution to this could be reorganizing the keys and leaving an area free of buttons at the lower part of the remote control—as suggested previously.

Improved Remote Control: The Final Result

Figure 9-15 shows some of the essential solutions identified to reduce the pain points for the TV remote control. As you have surely realized by now from my TV remote control design, I am a user experience expert and inventor, not an industrial designer. Still, the remote in Figure 9-15 does address many frustrations common among remote control users even today.

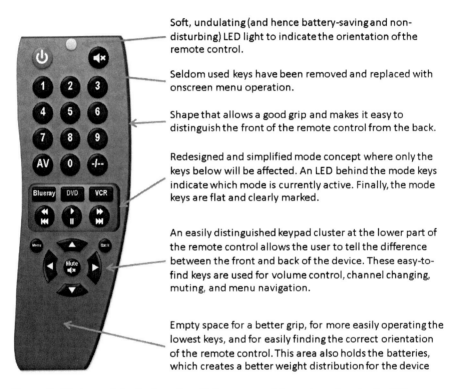

Soft, undulating (and hence battery-saving and non-disturbing) LED light to indicate the orientation of the remote control.

Seldom used keys have been removed and replaced with onscreen menu operation.

Shape that allows a good grip and makes it easy to distinguish the front of the remote control from the back.

Redesigned and simplified mode concept where only the keys below will be affected. An LED behind the mode keys indicate which mode is currently active. Finally, the mode keys are flat and clearly marked.

An easily distinguished keypad cluster at the lower part of the remote control allows the user to tell the difference between the front and back of the device. These easy-to-find keys are used for volume control, channel changing, muting, and menu navigation.

Empty space for a better grip, for more easily operating the lowest keys, and for easily finding the correct orientation of the remote control. This area also holds the batteries, which creates a better weight distribution for the device

Figure 9-15. Potential solutions for all the causes of the pain points in the TV remote control example

Step 5: Document the Results and Process the Output

There are certain places in this chapter's process and method where you can be diverted to a wrong track. Maybe the cause that you come up with for a pain point was wrong. It may also happen that the solution you designed to fix the pain point does not solve the problem—or creates new pain points.

Verifying the solutions is always essential. Verification can be done through usability tests, user interviews, or similar. You can find more inspiration on different ways of verifying solutions in Chapter 18.

You may also want to prioritize your solutions. Some pain points are more prominent than others. Some pain points will be noticed by all users, since they involve the core functionality of your web page, system, or device. Others may be noticed only by the few that use more advanced functionality. I would suggest focusing first on the pain points that most of your customers will experience, and then later focus on the pain points that fewer users experience.

Additionally, you may want to focus on the pain points that get the most negative feedback and areas where you have received the most complaints. These pain points may not be in the core flow of your product, but they may have a big negative impact on your user experience nevertheless.

Summary

This chapter has shown you how to find the pain points of your product, it has shown you how to find and verify the causes of the pain points, and it has given you tools to fix them.

As mentioned at the beginning of this chapter, fixing pain points may very well be a matter of life and death for your application, system, or device. Pain points really cause the end users a lot of pain, which they will have big difficulties forgiving.

Innovating Around First Impressions

The two previous chapters have given you tools to identify and hopefully fix the pain points of your current product, as well as to identify and innovate around your core tasks. These two methods are also essential for creating user experience innovation for the first impression that the users get from your website, device, or system.

The example I used in Chapter 9 on pain points was a TV remote control, which most end users will learn to use no matter how many pain points it has or how little the design is focused on the core tasks. That's because the need for watching TV is too strong. They may not buy a TV from the same manufacturer next time, but they will learn to operate at least the core functions eventually.

But what if you are designing a new website for which your market feedback tells you that users never come back after visiting the site the first time? What if you design a train ticket machine, but you notice that all the commuters queue up at the counter instead of using your machine? What if you design a calendar feature for your social website and find out that no one is using it?

First impressions—like when you meet another person (Figure 10-1)—will depend on a number of factors. They will depend on the look of your product, the screen layout (if any), the location, the attitude, and so on. If you are designing a device, first impressions will also depend on the so-called *out-of-the-box experience*: how the packaging looks, how easy it is to open, how many steps it takes to get the device working, and so on.

Also, the purchase experience (e.g., in a shop) and the way you choose to market your product is essential for first impressions. The first impression is very much about the expectations that the users have of your product, and hence on your brand, the product promise, and how you choose to market your product.

Figure 10-1. Example of first impression

Why First Impressions Are Important

I do not have data for this, but my claim is that the first impression of your product will last much longer than other experiences with your product. My claim is that if the first impression of your product is bad, then you will need at least ten brilliant user experiences later on to rectify this.

The problem is, however, that you may never be given the chance to show your ten great user experiences, since the users may already have chosen to leave your website or stop using your device or software package.

My theory can be backed up as follows: if you get a bad first impression of a person you meet, it will most likely take a lot of time for that person to convince you to like him or her. And in many cases you will not even give this person the chance to show another side of themselves.

In the remainder of this chapter I will go through the characteristics of a good first impression, followed by some tangible methods for innovating around the first impressions of your product.

Characteristics of a Successful First Impression

A user experience design with a successful first impression is characterized by a number of elements. These are described in the sections to follow.

Inviting and Simple

If you are designing a website, you want to make the initial front page inviting yet simple. You want to make the front page look professional and have a great design, but at the same time you want to give the users a good overview of what you are offering. But you also want to focus on the most-visited subpages (remember that if the user enters your website through a search engine, then she will most likely skip past your front page).

If you are designing a device, you want to make unpacking the device an easy and pleasant experience, as in Figure 10-2. You also want to make sure that the device is ready to use, without, for example, the user having to charge the device for a long time. You also want to make sure that the user can immediately start using the core tasks of the device.

Figure 10-2. The out-of-the-box experience is a key part of the first impression for devices and similar products.

If you are designing a piece of software, you want the start-up of your software to be fast, and the initial setup to be extremely easy. You also want to make sure that the installation is trouble free or even contains positive surprises (or wow).

In the train ticket machine example, you want to place the ticket machine in the right location; the physical design as well as the first screen should invite the users to use the machine. The right location may be next to the ticket counters, but it may also be inside the train, thereby avoiding the need for the user to ever miss his train due to buying a ticket.

Free of Pain Points

You want to remove all pain points from the initial use of your product. A good first impression is one that is free of pain. Apple, for example, is noted for the care they take in the packaging of their products, making even the unboxing experience into a wow event.

If your current website uses a Flash intro that for some users takes more than ten seconds or even minutes to load, you will surely need to fix that. You also want to look at how easy it is to get an overview of your website and how easy it is to find the core tasks.

If you are designing a device, you want to reduce or remove hurdles such as difficult unpacking and insertion of batteries. You want to avoid asking questions during start-up of the device, and so forth.

If you are designing a software package, then you want to avoid long and difficult-to-understand questionnaires and setup procedures before getting to the core of what your software can do. You certainly also want to look at removing pain points from the process of installing your software.

In the case of the train ticket machine, you want to remove any barriers that are preventing users from using the machine, such as where to find it, how to get started, how to choose language, and so on.

Core Tasks Are at the Center

The next things you should look at are the core tasks of your product. You want to make sure that when the user starts using your product, he can easily and quickly perform the core tasks.

If you are designing a website, you probably want to place the target users' core tasks right on the front page. If you are designing a low-cost mobile phone, you will want to lead the user directly to a place where he can perform core tasks like making a phone call, writing SMS, and so on.

In the case of the train ticket machine, you will have to look at whether the initial screen allows the user to immediately start his core task of purchasing a train ticket. You will also look at whether the user can perform the task of buying a train ticket for his desired destination in a shorter time and with a better experience than waiting in the queue for the counter.

Anecdote

If you have ever tried using train ticket machines in Germany, you will know how bad a first impression they give. The screens are very uninviting, it is highly illogical what to do as the first step, and you will find yourself taking as long five minutes to get a ticket for a specific train, slogging through five to ten cumbersome steps with questions about class and time of departure just to find out that the train is already full. On top of this, the payment procedure is very slow and the language of the machine will sometimes change from your initially selected English to German in certain situations. I always end up using ten or more minutes at these machines, after which I give up and join the long queue at the ticket counter.

Provide a Wow Factor

Adding positive surprises is another way to improve the first impression that the user gets of your product. Positive surprises can be many things, as you will learn in the next chapter. Positive surprises contribute mightily to a good first impression.

In the train ticket machine example, a positive surprise could be that the machine—based on, for example, face recognition or detection of your credit card—will suggest the purchase of a ticket to the same destination as the last time you rode. It might also remember which travel class you prefer to use, and so forth.

Method for Innovating Around First Impressions

The following sections will describe a concrete and straightforward approach to creating potentially successful user experience innovation around first impressions. In overview, the method consists of four steps:

1. Identify core tasks of your first impressions.

2. Identify pain points in your first impressions.

3. Innovate solutions.

4. Document results and process the output.

Throughout this chapter, I will use as an example a piece of word-processing software. I will assume that this software is sold as a DVD in a shop.

Step 1: Identify Core First Impression Tasks

The first thing you want is to identify the key elements that are part of the first impression of your product. You basically want to identify which core tasks the user needs to go through to get started using your product. I choose to define these as core tasks even though the user may only need to perform these tasks once (depending on your product). These tasks are core tasks since if the user does not succeed in performing them, then you will most likely already have lost a customer.

For a device you will hence list things like the packaging, the out-of-the-box experience, battery insertion and charging, and the experience when the product is first switched on. You will also need to look at the interaction of parts when the user first starts using your product as intended.

For a website you will list elements like the start screen, login functionality, initial Flash animations, basic layout, and navigation of your screen, as well as how the user gets to and executes the core tasks. For a piece of software, you will need to list download experience, or out-of-the-box experience if sold on CD/DVD. You also want to list the installation process, which is very often a hurdle for many users, and you want to consider the start-up time of your software and the first interactions the user needs to go through to start a core task.

The method for finding the core tasks around your first impressions is basically the same as that that described in Chapter 6. In this case, though, you will look solely to tasks that users need to go through the first time they unwrap and use the product.

Figure 10-5 shows a list of first impression elements for the example of the word-processing software.

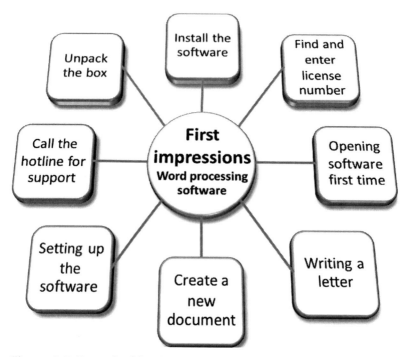

Figure 10-5. Example of first impression core tasks for a specific word-processing software package

Anecdote

When desktop computers first arrived on the scene in a big way during my college years, they were often equipped with a 5¼-inch floppy disk drive. I had quite a few fellow students who were at that time not yet confident with the computers, and one of these students one day tried to install new software on a university computer. The software was distributed on multiple floppy disks, and he followed the instructions displayed on the screen. When the first floppy disk was installed, the screen showed the message, "Please insert disk 2." And so he did. But the program didn't to tell him to remove disk 1, and he managed to fit two floppy disks into the drive, and only when trying to insert disk 3 did he realize the problem.

Step 2: Identify First Impression Pain Points

The next step is to identify which of the core tasks of your first impression includes pain points. You can use the same method as described in Chapter 9, but apply the method specifically to your first impression tasks.

You will want to identify in detail what each pain point is about (in the example in Figure 10-6 I have marked the problematic areas by underlining them).

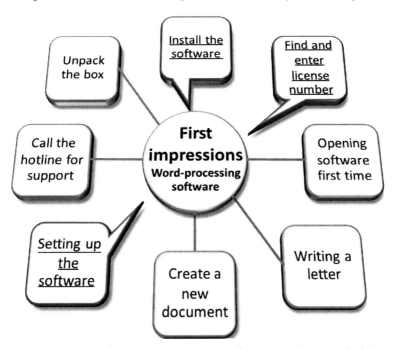

Figure 10-6. Identifying pain points in your first impression (marked in underline)

Step 3: Innovate Solutions

You now have the basis for innovating around the user's first-time experience. Again, you will want to gather a group of cross-functional team members and ideally some end users. Begin by reviewing your drawing (such as the one in Figure 10-6), or whatever other list of first impressions you have identified.

You may want to start with the pain points, but you may also likely find great user experience innovation around the core tasks. Figure 10-7 shows an example of the outcome of the innovation workshop around the core tasks and pain points for the first-time experience.

Figure 10-7. Example of result of innovation around first impression

Step 4: Document the Results and Process the Output

How you choose to document your results is up to you, but you will need to list all ideas and then verify them with target users. You may, for example, prototype them initially in simple ways and present them to target or lead users. Chapter 18 goes into detail about prototyping and verification.

Summary

This chapter has given you tools and methods to create successful user experience innovations for the first impressions that you are giving your users with your product. The first impression is extremely important, not only for products like websites where the user may leave within seconds if your first impression is not appealing, but also for every other type of product, including devices and software packages.

Creating Positive Surprises: The Wow Factor

Many productsproducts in this world are boring. They do what you expect them to do, but they never bring a smile to your face or make you laugh. As stated earlier, I compare product user experiences with the experience you get when you meet a person. If you go to a new dentist, you may be satisfied if he does the job of checking and fixing your teeth, but that won't necessarily make you want to come back to him again. Wouldn't it be great if he also tried to make you calm down by telling a joke, or by putting a nice painting in the waiting area? Wouldn't it be great if you actually liked the person behind the drill?

Being professional and focused but at the same time fun and playful is very seldom a negative combination of personalities for a person.

The same applies to products. You want the product to be professional, trustworthy, and easy to use. But if the product can also make you smile or laugh, you will be much more attached to that product. As Figure 11-1 illustrates, it's much better to give users a bit of the wow factor than to besiege them with pain points and frustration.

Anecdote

Many early phones from Nokia had a flat bottom because that was where a number of connectors were placed. The flat bottom made it possible for the phones to stand up on a table. The built-in vibration device in some products (due to space constraints inside the device) faced the opposite direction than was usual. This meant that if the phone was standing up and you received a call or SMS, the phone would start rotating while standing on the table. That rotation was later made into a design requirement. The first products did it unintentionally, but it made people smile, so a new requirement was born. It is easy to create pain points by accident. It is, however, more difficult to create positive surprises like this by accident.

Figure 11-1. Wow vs. frustration and pain points

The method described in this chapter is slightly different from the previous ones. This chapter's method focuses on adding small innovative surprises to the end user in essential places in your product. This method does not necessarily provide any new functionality or technologies to your device, system, or web page, but it may improve your user experience considerably, simply by giving the user a nice experience with the core parts of your product.

Adding small surprises or wows to your product is in some situations more important than actually adding new functionality or technologies. New functionality may take a long time for users to understand and learn, and new technologies may take several years to take off and to be adopted by users. Positive surprises (or wows) may on the other hand be immediately acknowledged and appreciated by your customers.

So why not focus on creating positive surprises (or wows) for the things you already have in your product? Why not try to create a great experience instead of frustration and pain points? A wow can simply be a good-looking graphical layout or funny icons. It can be the look or design of your device, or it can be small, intelligent features. A wow can be anything that brings unexpected delight to your users.

If you are designing a web page, positive surprises can be visual, in the form of graphics or structure. A feature that detects the language of the user could be a positive surprise. Sometimes it's enough to surprise the user that the web page simply provides the user with the information or functionality that the user wants. Another positive for a web page can be that it loads very fast.

If you are designing a device, a positive surprise can be that the battery is precharged, or it can be that everything is already set up and ready to be used. It can also be a hidden cool game on a device where you would never expect to find a game.

Anecdote

I started in the mobile phone industry in 1992, when some of the very first digital mobile phones were developed. At that time, the target users were businessmen, mainly since these devices had a price of around $2,000 and could more or less only place and receive calls.

The first mobile phone I worked on was the Hagenuk MT 900. It was equipped with a fully graphical display. That was at a time when segmented displays were the normal technology.

Over a single weekend and in my spare time, I implemented a Tetris game for the device, and showed a working version of it the following Monday. Even though playing games was not seen as a core task for the target users, the idea quickly gained traction inside the company, and the company decided to integrate the game into the next product, the Hagenuk MT-2000 (shown in Figure 11-2). The game was seen as a positive and unexpected surprise, and a large number of customers loved it. In this way I managed to bring the first game ever to a mobile phone.

Positive surprises very much depend upon the expectations of the user. If your competition is already doing something, it will be a lot more difficult (but not impossible) to turn your innovation involving the same thing into a positive surprise.

A general rule of thumb is that you should never create wow for its own sake. Unnecessary animations and design that slow down the core tasks of the user will easily turn into pain points.

Figure 11-2. Hagenuk MT-2000 (here in the Cetelco variant); the first ever mobile phone with a game

Characteristics

Positive surprises (or wows) can take many shapes and forms, but at their essence they leave users with a smile on their face or a good feeling inside.

They Bring a Smile

A positive surprise can, for example, happen via a small animation when a user opens a menu. A positive surprise can also come with a small, hidden feature that the user learns to use after a lot of experience with your program.

A wow is in nature very close to a positive surprise, but it will give the user an even more positive feeling. With a wow, the user may even say "great," "cool," or "wow" (not necessarily out loud, but at least in their own mind).

Often playfulness is a way to achieve wows and positive surprises.

Many people experience the wow feeling when they try a car that has a lot more horsepower than they are used to. Many experience wow when they return from a successful date or when their child takes its first steps. If you achieve these same feelings through your product, then you will have a very good chance of successful user experience innovation.

They Exceed Expectations

Positive surprises will very much depend on the expectations of your end users. For example, Apple customers will be highly disappointed if the user experience does not provide some level of wow. If you work at a company selling word-processing software, you may need to create more positive surprises and wow than the major players already ruling the market. If you are a newcomer in a mature market, such as the mobile device industry, you will want to raise the bar considerably for positive surprises and wow. Somehow, you need to exceed what your customers and users have come to expect. Only then can you surprise them.

They Are in the Open

One thing to realize is that placing a positive surprise or wow in a deeply hidden place or in a rarely used feature of your product will make only a very small percentage of your users surprised and happy; the surprise will not reach the majority of your users, and hence the effect of your efforts will be very limited. You want your surprises and wows to reach the majority of your users. You want to place the surprises in your core tasks and in where they will cause a good first impression.

They Cause No Pain

Creating surprises and wow in the core interaction without actually creating pain points is a very fine balance. Many user experience elements that have been designed and added to create a wow end up becoming serious pain points instead.

A great (or rather sad) example is the number of web pages with Flash intros (see Figure 11-3). While these may take just a few seconds to load on the designer's computer, they often take tens of seconds or even minutes to load for an average user.

As a general rule, positive surprises and wow should *never* be perceived as pain points, even for a small percentage of your users. For example, assume you've created an animation that plays when users open a new menu in your application. If users *think* the animation is slowing the loading of the menu, even if it's not, then you have created a perceived pain point. If many of your users believe that the animation is delaying the core task that they want to accomplish, your perceived pain point ends up becoming a *real* pain point.

Design your positive surprises and wows carefully—and within the core interaction of your product. Such innovations can move your system, device, or web page from average to premium.

Figure 11-3. When an attempt to create wow becomes a pain point

How to Wow

There are a number of methods to creating positive surprise and wows. You can create them through visual layouts and animations, you can create them by placing small treasures in your product, and you can even create them by building in intelligent solutions that surprise your users.

Visual Surprises and Wows

The most obvious—and common—way for many products to create positive surprises and wows is through visual communication: the layouts, icons, animations, images, and so on. For example, you can create visual surprises and wows by designing the layout of your web page simply, with easy-to-understand icons and a clear and easy overview. You can also add Flash animations, but as mentioned before, do so with great care.

If you are designing a device, you can create an outstanding physical design, you can create state-of-the-art graphics, and you can create logical visual flows for achieving the core tasks. If you are designing a piece of software, you can create a great layout for your application, innovative icons, cool animations, and so on—but of course you should consider the start-up time of your software.

Anecdote

The most successful web page in the world is Google's search page. But you certainly cannot say that Google has the most impressive visual experience. When Google launched its search engine, it basically had only two wows: the speed of loading the initial page (due to reduced graphics on the main page) and the speed at which it could find and return suitable and good search results.

I believe that Google has deliberately maintained its original, simple look for historical reasons and to communicate that your core task is its main focus. Google is hence a brilliant example of how you can create wow without focusing solely on the visual impression.

Playfulness

Playfulness is often an overlooked element of user experience design and innovation. Many influential people in your company (e.g., in management) take the products very seriously, and they will often argue that your product is designed for, for example, business purposes. But since when did business have to be boring?

Anecdote

What is the real value of Google Maps and Google Earth? Is it the fact that you can find a specific place or route, as shown in Figure 11-4[1]? No. I would claim that the real value of these products is in their playfulness. They are simply just fun to play around with. Seeing your childhood home becomes an attraction. Moving around in the world, perhaps by exploring satellite images, becomes fun.

---

[1] iStockPhoto®, ©Nikada, Weimar, Germany - March 31, 2011: A man using an Apple iPad with Google Maps, with a satellite view of New York City on the screen. The iPad, the digital tablet with the multitouch screen is produced by Apple. The software displayed is produced by Google.

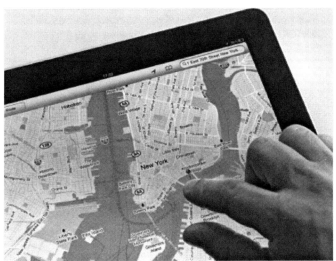

Figure 11-4. *Playfulness as a core element of the Google Maps user experience*
Source: iStockPhoto; copyright by Nikada (Weimar, Germany, March 31, 2011)

Playfulness can no longer be achieved simply by adding a small arcade game to a device or web page. Playfulness should ideally be an integral part of the entire user experience.

Playfulness will become an increasingly important competitive factor, not only for areas where user experience is already a focus (mobile devices, web pages, etc.), but also for products where there has traditionally been little or no focus on user experience (washing machines, word processors, hi-fi equipment for homes, medical devices, etc.). If you think that you are in a business where you do not need to look at playfulness, well then write me an e-mail and I will claim that you may be wrong.

Anecdote

Bang & Olufsen originally became famous for actually creating a design for—at that time—very dull-looking hi-fi equipment. The company later began to create not only state-of-art device designs, but also a number of mechanical and highly playful elements, such as CD doors that open automatically when a hand is in proximity of the device.

One classical invention was the fast-moving CD changer arm in the BeoSound 9000 6 CD player. Even when launched many years ago, it could have been possible to store the music electronically, so that the pause between playing two CDs could have become almost zero. That goal could have been achieved without moving the CD changer arm any more than 100 km/h. Instead, Bang & Olufsen chose to equip the device with the fastest-moving arm in the industry, and even made it visible through a glass plate, as shown in Figure 11-5. This is a great example of designing playful experiences—even when engineering solutions could have solved the same core task for the target user.

Figure 11-5. Bang & Olufsen BeoSound 9000. Copyright Bang & Olufsen. Used by permission

Hidden Treasures

Focusing only on creating surprises and wow around visual elements may not be sufficient. For many types of products, the visual appearance is where your competition will also go first, so you will want to innovate in other areas as well in order to stay ahead.

Another way to create positive surprises and wows is by innovating so-called *hidden treasures*. Hidden treasures cover a large variety of small surprises or wows that the user will find over time. Figure 11-6 shows an example of a small positive surprise on the carton for Innocent's Pure Fruit Smoothie drink.

Hidden treasures can also be shortcuts to often-used functions that the user may not realize in the beginning but will learn over time. Finding a faster way to accomplish a task can for many users be a very positive experience.

Figure 11-6. Positive surprise on Innocent smoothie carton.

Anecdote

Many years ago, when predictive text input was still very new, my nontechnical-minded brother started using the predictive text feature on his Nokia device—and he loved it. But one day he told me about a pain point. He felt that it was quite cumbersome to change the suggested word to another possible match.

I asked him how he did it. When the word was not correct, he would press the Options soft key and scroll all the way down to the function called "Next match." When I then told him about the shortcut for that functionality via the star key, he said, "Wow, that is so smart."

Actually, one could in this situation argue that getting the next match is a core task for many users and that the user experience of this core task was not initially designed well enough. That may well be true. However, with this specific user, his original pain point turned into a wow.

Hidden treasures can also be free downloadable games or other functionality that is gained as a reward when the user has used the product some time. Hidden functions that can be activated only through a secret code may also be seen as treasures, at least if your target users have a tendency to try to find and share such treasures. An example of a hidden treasure for a GPS-enabled mobile device could be the presentation of a free downloadable game or application when the user first enters a specific GPS location. For a social website it could be free credits when the user gets more than 100 friends.

An important thing to emphasize for hidden treasures is that you should never deliberately choose to initially hide functions needed to accomplish core tasks. Doing so will almost automatically create a pain point. But if you want to offer some extra goodies for certain passionate users, hidden treasures can provide a very attractive path.

Hidden treasures can also spread via viral marketing. For example, you may be able to find discussion forums where people share how to obtain these goodies. Thus, having the goodies will engender positive discussion of your product.

Again, do not hide or obstruct essential features. In my mind, a number of shareware software developers have gone way too far in hiding essential functionality until you purchase the product. Users have already gone through a cumbersome download and installation process, and they may become very dissatisfied and uninstall your software immediately if they cannot try out the product for real before purchasing. A time limit for the use may be a far better option in the case of shareware software. Don't obstruct the very reason to use your product in the first place.

Intelligence and Context Awareness

Intelligent behavior in your product can also provide users with positive surprises and wow. If your web page automatically detects the needed language to be used, this could be a convenient and positive surprise. However, make sure to not make it a pain point when your language guess is wrong. I have, for example, been travelling to Southeast Asia for a year now, and I am pretty fed up with Google always presenting me with texts in Thai, Filipino, or similar. But at least there is a shortcut and some text written in English to help me switch to English again. But why does the web page not remember my language selection the next time I visit it?

Concerning web pages, I see a potential for remembering not only your login information and your language preferences, but also for remembering the last task you were performing when you last exited the page. Why do social web pages discard my half-finished e-mails if I exit? Why can I not simply continue writing my e-mail when I enter the web page again?

Another example of intelligent positive surprises for a web page is when your web page learns the tasks that the user typically performs, and then makes it easier and faster to get to these tasks.

An example of user experience innovation intelligence for cars is remembering the seat angle settings when the user enters the car. For a train or bus ticket machine, an example of an intelligent wow could be a camera recognizing your face and suggesting tickets to the destinations where you have gone previously, just as the person behind the ticket counter may over time learn where you typically want to go. If you are designing a mobile device, the device may over time detect which functions you typically use, and then place a shortcut to these on your desktop.

When designing intelligent positive surprises and wows, you need to consider security issues and be very observant of privacy issues. Many users do not like systems that start changing things without warning. Seeing your entire history of previously visited web pages in your browser can be great for you, but maybe not so great for your wife or husband.

Some of what I've mentioned in this section relates to context awareness. That speaks to a product's ability to react differently depending upon the context in which it is used. You'll read more about that aspect of user experience in Chapter 16.

Methods for Innovating

You've just finished reading about how to create positive surprises in the sense of how and where to consider creating features in your product. That's the easy problem to solve, actually. The real question is this: How do you discover and decide which specific surprises to implement? Next we will look at several methods by which to answer that question.

Creating Positive Surprises and Wows for Core Tasks

To present positive surprises and wows that have a big impact, you want to place them where most of your users will see or experience them. Placing a wow for a function that is rarely used by any of your users will not give any impact. Thus, center your efforts around the core tasks of your product.

You can, for example, place each of your core tasks in the center of a diagram, and then place applications, technologies, user needs, pain points, and so on around it. You may not need a full list of applications and technologies around the core task; you can instead focus on areas where you already have an idea of where positive surprises or wows can be hidden. You may also want to list only user needs that are relevant to surprises and wows.

Figure 11-7 shows how such a list could look for a specific piece of video conversion software, where a core task has been identified around converting and transferring movies to mobile devices. In this figure I have placed user needs, technologies, pain points, and applications around this specific core task.

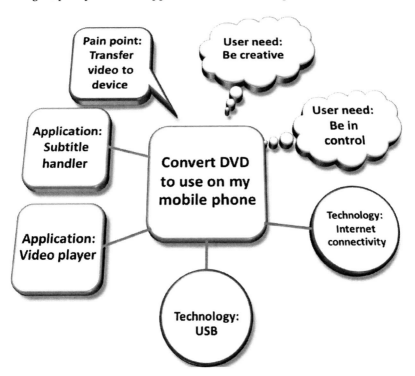

Figure 11-7. *Core task placed in the middle of the diagram for the video conversion software example*

Figure 11-8 shows how you can then invite a group of people with different expertise and ideally some lead users to a session to innovate for your specific product (in this example, a video conversion software package).

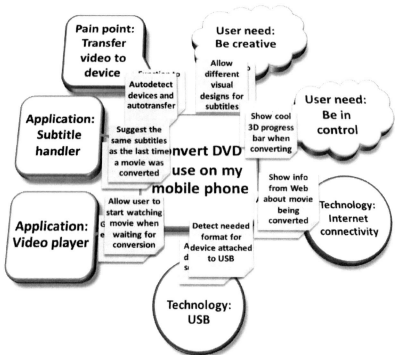

Figure 11-8. Example of results from innovating wow and positive surprises around the core task

Creating Positive Surprises and Wows for the First Impression

The first impression for many products, such as web pages and some types of software, is often where you will either get and keep a new customer, or lose the customer and never see them again. For all types of products, it is important to create positive surprises and wows around the first impressions.

Follow the method in Chapter 10 for innovating around first impressions. That method will help you place positive surprises and wows into the first impressions of your product. The first impression of your product is also a place to be sure not to create pain points, so—as mentioned before—be very observant about potential wows and surprises created around the first impression.

Avoid Unnecessary Wows

You must achieve a balance between providing positive surprises and wows on one hand, and on the other hand making sure not to be too clever. Remember that the difference between a wow and a pain point is often paper thin. A surprise element that is seen by 60 percent of users as a wow and 20 percent of users as a pain point should be redesigned or reconsidered.

Too much visual wow on your web page may easily become a pain point if the user believes that it slows down performing his core tasks. Hidden treasures may be a pain point if you, for example, choose to hide core functions. Overly intelligent solutions may intimidate a large number of your users and might make them dislike your product. Avoid creating surprises that might be perceived as pain points.

Summary

Creating positive surprises and wows is an essential part of successful user experience innovation, but it is also a difficult exercise where you need to balance creating true wows and pain points. If you follow the methods and guidelines described in this chapter, you may potentially come up with things that truly make your product stand out.

Innovating Around an Ecosystem

If you are designing a product, it is tempting to focus on the core of your product only. However, a lot of successful user experience innovation has been done *around* the core product. Here are some examples:

- If you are designing a mobile device, you can create user experience innovation by providing great tools for your PC or the Internet that can be used to extend or support the user experience of your device. You will look at successful service providers and maybe ask permission to use their services.

- If you are designing a social web page, you can look at how to integrate services from other web pages, or you can make it very easy for your customers to transfer account data, friend lists, and so forth from a competing social web page. You can also look at how to integrate your services in a great way for mobile devices.

- If you are designing video conversion software, you could look at how to download alternative subtitles from the Internet and how to easily connect your computer to a TV.

    The trick is to not limit your definition of your product to the actual product itself; rather, you should see your product as whole ecosystem.

Anecdote

When the Apple iPod was launched in 2001 (see Figure 12-1), it got a lot attention due to its design and the basic user experience of the product itself, but it did not become really successful until the entire ecosystem (e.g., with the iTunes music store and the iTunes PC application) was put into place in 2003. My view is that the real reason for the success of the iPod was the superior user experience of the ecosystem that was built around the iPod.

Most competitor music devices at that time supported a USB connection. However, buying and transferring music was a cumbersome process. The process was also cumbersome if the user wanted to convert and transfer her existing CD music collection to the device. The iPod and the surrounding ecosystem removed all those pain points.

Apple's ecosystem has over the years and with the introduction of the iPhone and iPad been successfully extended by Apple to cover applications as well as music. The ecosystem is highly successful now, and includes movies, games, music, lifestyle and productivity applications, and so forth. A large part of the success of the iPhone, not least when it comes to application downloading, is due to Apple's existing and (for the users') well-known and appreciated ecosystem.

Figure 12-1. The first iPod

Introducing the Method

The method of innovating around your ecosystem consists of the following steps:

1. Identify target user needs and potential future core tasks.

2. Identify your potential ecosystem.

3. Draw your ecosystem.

4. Innovate around your ecosystem.

5. Document and process the results.

Throughout this chapter I will use an e-book reader application as an example. We will assume that this e-book reader is already available for Internet tablets and PCs.

Step 1: Identify Target User Needs and Potential Future Core Tasks

As with all user experience innovation, you need to know who your customers are and what their current and latent needs are. And you will need to know which tasks the user would like to achieve with your product. You will also want to know the pain points, because some of your pain points may actually derive from your current ecosystem rather than from your product.

By examining the target users' needs, core tasks, and pain points, you will be able to identify the *potential* ecosystem of your product. And based on this you will be able to create potentially successful user experience innovations.

Step 2: Identify Your Potential Ecosystem

The first thing you want to do is to identify your ecosystem. This step is not only about identifying your current ecosystem, but very much also about identifying your *potential* ecosystem.

If you are designing a social website, you may want to look at how to integrate features from (maybe competing) social websites, from weather forecast providers, from existing online calendar applications, and so forth. You may want to look at providing dedicated PC or mobile device applications that may improve or extend the experience of your website.

If you are designing a remote control device, you will need to look at potential accompanying PC software for setting up the remote control and potential Internet services to help the user out. For example, if your remote control is for a TV, you might want to design onscreen menus that allow the user to personalize the remote control.

If you are designing a mobile device, you will need to look at the entire ecosystem involving how the user downloads new applications to the device; how the user edits, backs up, and shares contacts via a PC or the Internet; and so forth.

If you are designing a piece of PC software, you will need to look at how integration with your Internet-based services (e.g., templates, settings, and similar) can easily be applied. You will also need to look at applying your PC software to specific physical devices, such as mobile phones. And you will need to look at how you can potentially integrate your solutions with other PC software.

I have deliberately avoided using the phrase *thinking outside the box* previously in this book, since that term has been misused to cover so many different things. But in this case you really need to think outside of the box. And in this case your box is the specific product—or sometimes even part of the product—that you are designing. And *outside of the box* can refer to many things—from obvious ecosystem elements to the fridge in the user's kitchen. You need to see your device, system, or web page from a much bigger perspective.

You need to be very open-minded when thinking about your potential eco-system, but you also need to restrict yourself. Potentially any product in this world could communicate with a fridge, a coffee machine, or an Internet service, but you need to keep your focus on the *relevant* ecosystem elements.

A good general approach to identifying and prioritizing your ecosystem ele-ments is to invite a group of people for a meeting specifically to identify those ele-ments. As always, you should also invite users to this session, and in this case lead users would be an obvious choice, since these users may be able to think outside of the box for your product.

Following, I will go through concrete approaches to identifying and prioritizing your ecosystem elements.

User Needs for Identifying Ecosystem Elements

To identify the relevant ecosystem elements you should use the user needs of your target users. User needs will often reveal potential and uncovered ecosystem ele-ments of your product.

If you are designing an Internet tablet, the user needs may, for example, reveal the need for easily downloading or streaming music. And you should hence include music download and music streaming to your ecosystem. If you are designing a piece of word-processing software, user needs may reveal that the users have a need to perform spreadsheet functions, and you would hence add spreadsheet applica-tions to your ecosystem. And so forth.

In the example of an e-book reader application, the user needs include the ability to get a new book when finished with the last book, and hence book publish-ers for e-books should be added to the ecosystem. Actual authors of novels, litera-ture, poems, and so on would also be added.

Another need for the target users of the e-book reader is the ability to read a book even when commuting to and from work. Hence adding mobile devices to the ecosystem is natural.

A third user need identified for the e-book reader is that users would love to have their reading experience enhanced—for example, with music and background images. This means that music providers and image providers are added to the ecosystem.

Core Tasks for Identifying Ecosystem Elements

Also, ,the core tasks can help you identify and prioritize your ecosystem. If the user has several core tasks that are poorly covered or not covered by your product, then these are very important ecosystem elements.

If you are designing a smart phone, you may find out that downloading a new application to the device is a core task. So you should add application providers and probably also application developers to your ecosystem. If you are designing a video conversion application for PCs, you may find out that burning a DVD disc is a core task, and if your software does not already support this, you will want to add it to your ecosystem.

In the case of the e-book reader application, one of the identified core tasks is printing the book. Hence printers are added to the ecosystem.

Pain Points for Identifying Ecosystem Elements

Finally, ,pain points often reveal elements of your ecosystem, especially those elements where the current solutions are not good enough.

If you are designing a mobile device, you might identify a pain point around connecting to the Internet, and you will hence include the network operators' handling of Internet connections as part of the ecosystem. If you are designing an LCD TV, and users report that setting up the channels is a hurdle, then you might decide that a PC interface and application should be part of your ecosystem. If the TV is able to connect to the Internet, you could also add web services to your ecosystem.

With the e-book reader example, it has been identified that the fonts used for displaying the text are hard to read. Hence font providers are added to the ecosystem.

Step 3: Draw Your Ecosystem

When you have identified, categorized, and prioritized your ecosystem elements, you are ready to create a simple drawing of your ecosystem on a whiteboard or similar.

Figure 12-2 shows how a drawing might look for the e-book reader application.

Step 4: Innovate Around Your Ecosystem

You are now basically ready to innovate user experience improvements for your ecosystem. Again, you want to invite a group of people (including, e.g., lead users) to an open innovation session.

As mentioned earlier, innovating around your ecosystem requires you to get out of your box. You will need to think how you can improve the interfaces in various parts of your ecosystem, and you might even want to remain open to entirely new sources of content for your product. You might even suggest including functionality from third-party software developers or web pages.

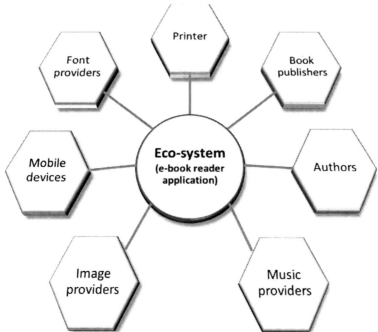

Figure 12-2. Ecosystem for the e-book reader application

User Needs, Core Tasks, and Pain Points

A concrete method to start innovating around your ecosystem is to directly apply target user needs, core tasks, and pain points to each of the identified ecosystem elements, and try to come up with truly innovative solutions for these needs, tasks, and pain points. You will be surprised at how these elements can also be extremely useful for user experience innovation for your ecosystem.

Displaced Simplicity

Another possibility is to use a method called *displaced simplicity*. Displaced simplicity refers to using an alternative platform or software product to solve a task that may be complex to solve with your own product.

If you are designing a mobile device, you might for example want to move complex tasks to PC software. If you are designing a remote control for a TV, you can move complex setup of the remote control to onscreen menus on the TV. If you are designing a PC application, such as an e-book reader, you might choose to displace complex functions to a supporting web page. And so forth.

When displacing functionality to another platform, it is seldom a good idea to simply copy the original functionality to the other platform. For users to actually spend the time and effort to use a different platform, you have to provide a true benefit for them. Simply moving your original functionality or copying the same interaction to another platform without any obvious reason or benefit may end up introducing a pain point instead.

E-book Reader Example

In the case of the e-book reader, the result of the innovation session could end up looking as shown in Figure 12-3.

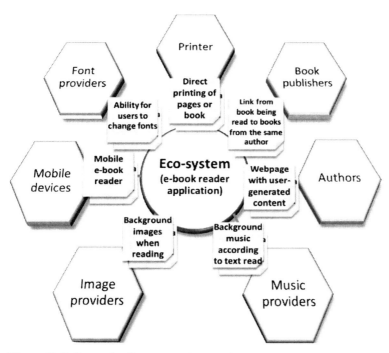

Figure 12-3. Example of ecosystem innovation

Step 5: Document and Process the Results

Documenting your results can be done in many ways, but verifying the results with end users is essential. In the case of involving third-party elements, you may also want to verify your results with third-party companies and interest groups.

You may also want to prioritize the user experience innovations found around the ecosystem. This is an important task, since fixing elements in the ecosystem can be extremely difficult, as certain factors will often be more or less out of your hands. But even difficult ecosystem innovations should be considered if they will have a big impact on the user experience.

Summary

Innovating user experience around the ecosystem can be challenging, but it can also provide you with truly successful user experience innovation. Some of your best user experience innovations may be around your ecosystem.

Innovating with Lead Users

The traditional method for innovation is to first find the needs of the users and then return to the company to create innovations within a team of colleagues. But why not involve the users in the innovation process?

However, you cannot ask just any user to be creative. The vast majority of users will only be able to explain where they have problems with your product, what their specific needs are, and what functions they use.

You need to find lead users. Lead users are characterized by creatively using your or competitive products. You might be able to find users who already design their own applications for your device, system, or web page. You might be able to find users who have already found their own workarounds for their needs with your product. You also might be able to find users who write blogs about how you or the competition could improve the products.

The steps for lead user innovation are as follows:

1. Find lead users

2. Prepare for a lead user workshop

3. Run the workshop

4. Document your results and process the output

The sections to follow provide tangible approaches to creating successful user experience innovations with your lead users.

Intellectual Property and Secrecy Concerns

Many companies are concerned about workshops being held with end users due to intellectual property rights and secrecy issues. Such concerns can, however, be solved by agreeing with the users before the workshop and by using nondisclosure agreements. Creating those agreements may require that you involve your legal department to prepare the necessary documents.

Step 1: Find Lead Users

Lead users can be found in several ways. You may already know a few of them from your company's complaint hotline. Or you can find them via the Internet by looking for people who have created their own small improvements to your product. Or you will find them by looking through the logs of official e-mail to your company.

You can also use an agency to find suitable lead users, and you can even ask a professional facilitator with user experience background to do your preparations and to run the workshop. This may be a good idea, at least the first time, for learning the tricks, but it will also be more expensive.

Instead of seeing these users as menace to your company who spam your in-boxes and hotlines, invite them for a creative workshop. These people will in many cases take two days out of their calendar just to be with you—for free! Of course, you should give them compensation if they need to stay in a hotel, and so on, but otherwise these customers usually come almost free of charge, and it is very wise to use their insights and creativity.

Anecdote

At Nokia, we ran an innovation project for physically challenged people. Initially we were unaware of the problems that some people with disabilities had using mobile devices. We were also unaware of how much these people actually relied on their mobile devices. The mobile device was often their main communication tool to the outside world—for chatting, socializing, finding their way around, requesting assistance, and so on.

We invited a group of 11 lead users for a workshop, together with our cross-functional team of industrial designers, user interaction experts, software developers, mechanical engineers, and so on. Not only were the lead users all involved in developing their own solutions for mobile devices, but they were also characterized by all being physically challenged.

The workshop was a true eye-opening experience. Finding accommodation in Copenhagen for blind people and people in wheelchairs was in itself a huge challenge. Finding a restaurant that could accommodate wheelchairs and where hearing-impaired people would not be disturbed by the acoustics was another huge challenge. I personally spent more than one week just making the practical arrangements for this workshop. I was forced directly into the problems that people with physical challenges have. And that in itself was extremely inspiring for me.

We had sign-language translators in the room for the two hearing-impaired people. During breaks, those members used their mobile devices to communicate with their friends through video calls. The member without arms would eat breakfast, lunch, and dinner with his feet. The blind member typed on his mobile device to take notes and write down ideas. The workshop not only produced a large number of concrete ideas, but it also revealed many specific user needs for these target user groups.

Figure 13-1 shows an example of a lead user. Your lead users may however, be completely different.

Figure 13-1. A lead user

Step 2: Prepare for the Workshop

Apart from the practical arrangements for the workshop, you will want to ensure a good location for it, with lots of room and tools to enhance creativity. You can do the preparations yourself, and perhaps learn quite a lot about your lead users in the process, or you can have, for example, a user experience practitioner do the work for you.

When inviting users, you do not want them to feel overwhelmed, so do not invite the entire company of 100 people to meet with 2 lead users. A good distribution is around 50 percent lead users and 50 percent people from your company.

If you are planning a workshop that will run for two or more days, one idea is to have the colleagues who are not participating in the workshop be on standby for some evening work. You can ask these colleagues to create demos or prototypes of the ideas that came up during the lead user workshop. These ideas can then be presented and discussed on the following day. This will speed up the innovation process, and you will get instant feedback on your ideas. And it will surely impress your lead users.

You also want the lead users to prepare for the meeting. You can for instance ask the lead users to prepare for presenting five specific needs that they have, five of their most prominent core tasks, and five pain points. To make it easier for them, you can prepare templates that describe each of the terms and provide spaces for the users to list their answers (e.g., as shown in Figure 13-2).

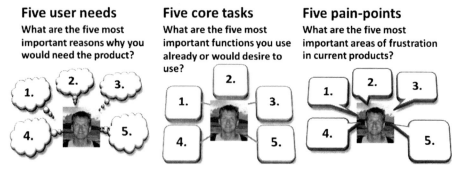

Five user needs

What are the five most important reasons why you would need the product?

Five core tasks

What are the five most important functions you use already or would desire to use?

Five pain-points

What are the five most important areas of frustration in current products?

Figure 13-2. Template for lead users to prepare before the workshop

Step 3: Run the Workshop

Now it's time to run the workshop, as illustrated in Figure 13-3. One advantage of doing innovation with users is that it gives you a good chance of designing things that actually cover a real user need. You can also verify your solutions quickly, since you can ask the users questions right away.

Figure 13-3. Example of a lead user workshop

Another advantage is that your users will likely come up with quite different solutions than you do. You may be stuck in a company- or technology-driven mindset that the lead users do not have.

Finally, during the workshop you can identify user needs and core tasks that you might have difficulty finding in an interview. During the workshop you can focus your innovations around the specific needs, core tasks, and pain points of the lead users that you invited, or you can use general needs for the target users as the basis of your innovations. But keep in mind that users generally will want to solve their own problems rather than somebody else's.

A structured approach during the workshop is to create innovations for the five user needs, core tasks, and pain points that each of the lead users have prepared. For further details on specific methods for this, refer to Chapter 4 for identifying user needs, and Chapters 6 and 9 for innovating around core tasks and pain points, respectively.

At the end of the workshop, you can spend some time with your lead users to prioritize the solutions and ideas that were created, thereby reducing (but not eliminating) the need for subsequent verification of your solutions. When prioritizing, you should listen to the users' opinions, but you can also contribute with feasibility evaluations, and so on.

Step 4: Document the Results and Process the Output

After the workshop, you should document all the user experience innovation ideas that came out. You may also want to prototype the most prominent potential ideas to verify with further target users. For more details on prototyping and verifying ideas, please refer to Chapter 18.

Summary

Lead user workshops can provide you with unique user experience innovation ideas that may never have come up inside your organization or company. Lead users will also give you very rapid feedback on your solutions, which otherwise could take weeks to get.

Lead user workshops are valuable for any kind of product or target user group, and in particular if you do not yet have deep insights into the needs, core tasks, and pain points of your current users—or if you are targeting a new group of target users.

Copying with Pride

Successful user experience innovations are rarely characterized by being first to market, but rather by being *done right*. In other words, innovations become successful when the user experience is great. Copying your competitors or other businesses is a great opportunity to create successful user experience innovation. But when copying, you really need to focus on doing it *right*.

The steps are pretty straightforward. You first need to *find* user experience innovation in competitor products, and then you need to improve these to make them successful. The methods for making the innovations successful are not much different from those described in previous chapters. The four steps needed for creating user experience innovation around competitor solutions are as follows:

1. Identify potential solutions from a competitor product.

2. Categorize competitor solutions.

3. Innovate solutions.

4. Verify solutions.

Anecdote

In the beginning of the mobile phone era, phones were most often operated using keypad buttons for each of the functions. Some devices used a function key that, when pressed at the same time as a digit key, would bring up a menu or execute a function (just like a shortcut on your computer). These devices were highly complex to use.

There were a few user experience pioneers, though, who invented the use of soft keys for mobile phones. You may be thinking Nokia, but that is wrong. The first mobile phones with soft keys came from either Siemens or Cetelco/Hagenuk. Even I am not sure who gets the real credit for the initial innovation, and I have worked with both companies. But it was for sure not Nokia. Nokia launched its first soft key–enabled device (the 2110) in 1994 and it was a big success, even though the first devices with soft keys came out in 1992. Figure 14-1 shows the Hagenuk MT 900.

Even at that time, the soft key concept was wasn't new. It existed for some very technical devices, such as oscilloscopes, but Siemens and Cetelco/Hagenuk were the first to bring it to the mobile phone market.

Even though Nokia was not the biggest mobile phone manufacturer at that time (it was number 3 after Motorola and Ericsson), it managed with the 2110 and its following products to make users and the industry believe that the soft key concept was invented by Nokia. Remember that history rarely remembers those who were first to do something; it usually remembers those who were first to do it right. (Admittedly, the fact that the Nokia 2110 was half the size and weight of the Cetelco/Hagenuk device probably had an influence here also.)

Figure 14-1. Hagenuk MT 900 with soft keys, from 1992. Created by Cetelco/Hagenuk. Photos used with permission from vintagemobilephones.com.

Step 1: Identify Potential Solutions from a Competitor Product

Identifying solutions from competitors takes some practice. Obvious great innovations are easy to spot, but sometimes you will also want to identify small and maybe hidden solutions that are easy to overlook. You also want to find solutions that may not make sense at first glance, but if used in another context may be really innovative. In the following sections, I will elaborate on how you can find solutions from competitor products.

Use Competitors' Products

Many designers and engineers tend to mainly use the products of their own company. If you are designing mobile devices, you might even be requested by the management to use only products from the company.

This is a big mistake. If you want to learn about competition, you should use its products. If you are designing a word processor, you should try to use a competing product for at least one or two months. If you are designing a website, you should follow the trends and improvements that your competition is following.

Finding user experience innovation is sometimes very easy (e.g., a new and innovative method to scroll a menu), and other times it may be quite tricky. Maybe you notice a small function in a calendar application that can become very useful if applied to a messaging application. Maybe you see a function in a piece of word-processing software that will make a lot of sense on your website.

Twisting these competitor ideas take a bit of practice as well. Which is why using competitor products should be a must for everyone related to innovation in the company. If you work at a company or organization that wants to invest in future user experience innovation, you should start allowing and encouraging your employees to use competitor products.

Competitor Intelligence

Larger companies may have specific teams or functions to look at what the competition is up to. This can make sense as long as competitor intelligence is also part of the innovation process.

In my opinion, competitor intelligence and teardown should be things that everyone in the company is involved in. Of course, you can certainly centralize some of the work of gathering and compiling data, and you can also centralize the purchase of competitor products.

The reason for actually using competing products is simple: you need to try functions, applications, and features yourself to see where potential successful user experience innovations may be hidden.

LCD TV Example

In this chapter, I will assume that you are designing an LCD TV. In such a case, you might choose to list solutions from a single competitor or brand. Figure 14-2 shows an example of documenting solutions for a specific competitor LCD TV. The solutions cover features, applications, design, and other potential elements of the product.

Figure 14-2. Example of potential solutions found on competitor LCD TV

Step 2: Categorize Competitor Solutions

The first thing you want to do with the solutions you have found in the competitor product(s) is to categorize them. You can, for example, try to identify which solutions solve a core task, whether the competitor solutions have pain points, and so on. I chose to distinguish between the following four categories of competitor solutions:

- Solutions that cover core tasks but are hidden

- Solutions that cover core tasks but have moderate or serious pain points

- Solutions that aren't part of a core task but have nice visual design

- Solutions that aren't part of a core task but have some interesting interaction elements

Depending on the nature of your product, you may need more categories, but determining whether the solution covers a user need (core task) is essential.

Step 3: Innovate Solutions

You are now ready to start innovating user experience solutions based on the categories of the identified solutions from your competitor device. Following are some ways to innovate for different categories of solution.

Solutions That Cover Core Tasks but Are Hidden

Figure 14-3 illustrates a hidden function in a competing product. In this case, your innovation process is straightforward. The function is a core function that you have identified as a core task. The competitor has maybe created a brilliant solution for a core task, and the only thing you need to do is adapt it to your product and make it visible. However, in many cases the solution may not be directly applicable to your product, or you may need to be concerned about copyrights.

So, no matter how brilliant the solution of your competitor is, you will still want to innovate around the solution just as if it was a core task that you just identified. Doing so may very likely give you a solution that is even better than that of your competitor.

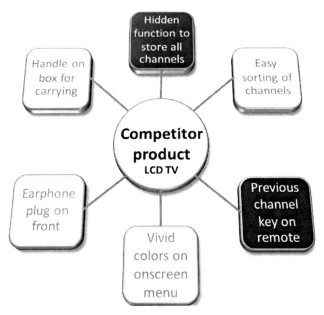

Figure 14-3. Hidden competitor core tasks marked with black

In the LCD TV example, the following solutions were identified to belong to this category:

- *Hidden function to store all channels:* Saving TV channels is a core task when it comes to the first use of the product, and when TV stations are added or removed. The teardown of the competitor TV revealed a pretty intelligent autostore function, but it was hidden away in a very illogical way.

- *Previous channel key on remote*: Switching between two channels is a core task for many TV viewers, but the placement and icon used in the competitor product was difficult to understand.

The initial step could be to simply copy the functions and make them more visible for the TV that you are designing, but as mentioned it may make a lot of sense to use some of the previously discussed methods for innovation around core tasks also.

Following I will list a few examples of how a competitor solution can spawn new and innovative user experience ideas:

- Hidden function to store all channels:

- You may choose to store channels in the user's language in the first channel locations. This can be achieved by detecting the country code transmitted for (some) TV channels and pairing this with the selected menu language.

- You can store channels according to the number displayed in the TV station logo by using the powerful image-processing abilities of the LCD TV.

- You can capture and store the logo for each channel (typically shown in upper-right corner of the TV screen) and use this in other core functions (e.g., the channel overview menu).

- You can detect the actual sound of the TV station and interpret the language being spoken on it. This will require some processing and language detection software, but it's doable.

- Previous channel key on remote:

- You can allow the user to easily swap between two or more channels.

- You can bring up an onscreen menu allowing the user to switch between the five most recently visited channels.

- You can offer a new key on the remote control that allows the user to switch between the five most watched TV channels (based on the total time spent watching each TV channel).

Solutions That Cover Core Tasks but Have Moderate or Serious Pain Points

Figure 14-4 highlights some solutions that cover core tasks, but are implemented in ways that bring pain to the user. Solutions in this category may cover core tasks that you overlooked in your user interviews or research. They might be potential future core tasks in your product.

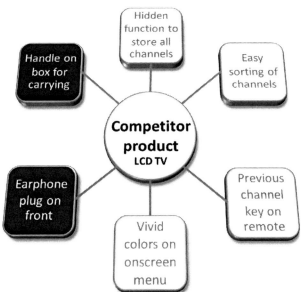

Figure 14-4. Competitor core tasks with pain points marked with black background

If you can identify a potential future core task, you have a good chance at creating a successful user experience innovation. In the LCD TV example, the following solutions were categorized as core tasks with serious pain points:

- *Handle on box for carrying*: Carrying a large LCD TV is a main pain point for many users. The competitor TV was equipped with a handle that was very sharp and small.

- *Earphone plug on front*: The competitor chose to place the earphone plug on the front of the TV, which ruined the visual experience.

Again, the easy approach could be to simply copy the solutions while fixing the pain points; or you can—as I recommend—choose to create further user experience innovation around these pain points, as described in Chapter 9. If you use these methods, you may, for example, come up with these additional solutions:

- Handle on box for carrying:
- You can mount a large handle or even two handles on the box, making it possible for two people to carry the TV.
- You can add two small, cheap wheels on the bottom of the box, and a handle on the top by which to pull the TV behind you.
- Earphone plug on front:
- You can hide the earphone plug behind a small, nicely designed panel.

- You can place a USB port and/or a card reader behind the panel so that the user can look at photos or similar on the TV.

- If you are designing a high-end TV, you can consider letting the panel open electronically when the user moves a hand in front of it.

- You can add lighting around each of the connectors and make this element a part of the visual design of your TV. This will also allow the user to find the plugs in darkness.

Solutions That Aren't Part of a Core Task but Have Nice Visual Design

Figure 14-5 shows a function that is not part of performing a core task, but that represents an attractive visual design element. Functions like this may catch your attention—for example, a menu that scrolls in an elegant way, a device that has some tasteful split lines, or a good-looking solution for a display frame.

The competitor is—luckily—not using these solutions for core tasks, and hence these most likely will not become successful user experience innovations for the competitor. You can look at the basic ideas, redesign them, and apply them to some of the core tasks of your own device.

You may also want to innovate further around the idea. For this purpose, you can use the previously described innovation method for technologies (if the visual element is driven by, e.g., a new method for scrolling) or for applications (if the identified solution on the competitor device can be characterized as an application).

In the LCD TV example, let us assume that this solution was identified only on the competitor's sound menu. If you really like this concept from your competitors, you may now want to bring it to all of your onscreen menus. Or you can innovate around this technology and, for example, come up with the following additional ideas:

- You can allow the user to personalize the colors of the menu (e.g., by allowing the user to select different themes). You should design a transparent theme also, since this is a solution that many users will need (if you have ever tried entering a menu to fix something when the spouse or kids are watching their favorite program, you will know about this need).

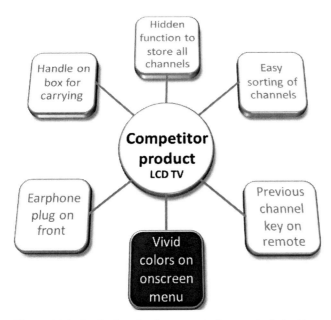

Figure 14-5. A solution that's not part of a core task, but has a nice design

- As a spin-off idea, you may want to allow the user to personalize the subtitles. With digital TV reception, the subtitles are received as text strings, and hence it is up to the TV to display the subtitles in an adequate way. So why not allow a visually impaired person to see subtitles in a very large font? Why not allow other users to use fully transparent subtitles? Why not allow users to adapt the background color to match the furniture? For some users (e.g., the visually impaired), these may represent core tasks, but for others they may not. But these solutions could possibly trigger some positive surprises or wow.

- As a further spin-off, you may allow the user to store and later use the subtitles.

Solutions That Aren't Part of a Core Task but Have Some Interesting Interaction Elements

Figure 14-6 shows a solution that is a nice idea but doesn't really cover a user need. Other such examples might include the handling of the scrolling from one page to the next, the text-entry method, and the keypad layout.

This is the situation where you identify other nonvisual but interesting user experience design elements in a competitor's product. The solution on the competitor device is not a part of a core task, so this gives you the chance to take the solution, redesign it, create further innovations, and then apply those to one or more core tasks in your own device.

In this case you would most likely use the technology and core task innovation methods described earlier. You can view the interaction element as a technology and find suitable applications to add it to, but you also need to be very focused on applying the solution to your core tasks.

In the case of the LCD TV, the easy-sorting-of-channels solution has been put in this category. Sorting channels should not be a core task for the end users if you've designed your channel-autostoring features correctly, but in many TVs today it still is.

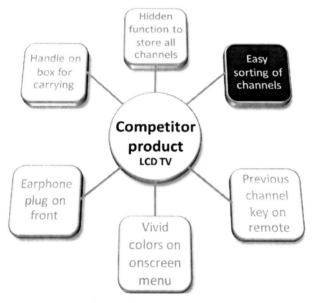

Figure 14-6. A solution that doesn't cover a user need, but is still a nice idea

The solution in the competitor product allows users to first mark one channel to move, after which the user can specify where to place the marked channel. The competitor's solution allows the user to insert a channel between two other channels. Your current solution allows only the swapping of channels, which has been identified as a pain point since it makes it very cumbersome to organize the list, as the user always ends up having to move a channel other than the one desired.

In this case the obvious solution is to copy your competitor's handling. You may want to improve the handling by visually indicating that the user is inserting the channel in between two other channels.

If you, for example, use the technology innovation method described in this book, you may also come up with other places where you can apply similar handling. If you are using the method described for core tasks, you might invent new user experience solutions, such as marking multiple channels for moving at the same time. Or you might use a more visual and maybe two-dimensional method for moving channels around—for example, using a screenshot from the TV station or the TV station logo as the icon for each channel.

Step 4: Verify Solutions

When you have found suitable twists on competitor solutions, you will need to verify these, as described in more detail in Chapter 18. You will want to make sure that you are covering true end-user needs, that you have not created pain points, and that your solution is highly usable.

Concerns

When you are twisting and improving solutions, you want to make sure that you are not infringing on any intellectual property rights. Avoid blindly copying any competitor technologies (including, e.g., visual design), as this may violate copyrights.

If you insist on, for example, using a patented solution, you can sometimes find workarounds to avoid infringing on the patent. Many patents involving user interaction are defined very narrowly, and you may be able to create a solution that does not infringe on the rights (and is even better than the original).

Note that you cannot create a patent for a generic solution to a problem—only for a specific method to perform a certain task or to achieve a certain goal. If you focus on looking at what problem a specific feature of a competitor is solving, and then design your own approach to solve this problem, you will rarely infringe on any copyrights or patents.

And of course, you can purchase a license for a specific patent if you really want to use the specific methods covered by the patent.

Summary

As indicated in this chapter, you can successfully copy ideas from your competition, or from other products in other industries. This chapter has also covered how to apply different innovation methods depending on the characteristics of the solution you have found in the competitor product.

When you use these methods for copying, you will automatically learn about twisting solutions and creating innovations for your own products. Copying solutions from your competitors is nothing to be ashamed of. Every company does, sometimes even without knowing it.

As mentioned, it's important to look to improve upon solutions that your competitors just haven't gotten right. These are low-hanging fruit. However, you can also innovate further around the solutions of your competitors, which will likely allow you to come up with other successful user experience innovations.

Copying with Pride

One can argue that it is not true innovation if you copy an idea from an existing product, redesign it, and start marketing it. However, if magazines, analysts, and consumers *perceive* it as innovation, then it *is*. And it may well turn out to be a successful one.

CHAPTER 15

Innovating Around Paradoxes

Looking at paradoxes is another excellent method for creating user experience innovation. If you, for example, see the need for security on your website as essential among your target users, but you are at the same time dealing with target users who have a profound need for simplicity, this may be a paradox that you would like to focus on. The need for both simplicity and security is a common paradox. Following are some general examples of paradoxes you might encounter:

- If you a designing video-editing software, users will often demand more functionality, but they will also suffer from an increased number of functions.

- If you are designing a device for physically challenged people who at the same time want a modern-looking product, you may be faced with a paradox.

- Users may have a need to know where they are, but at the same time not desire that other people know where they are.

- Your news website may be funded primarily by banner commercials, but the end users mainly want to read the news.

Paradoxes can be caused by conflicting user needs, or they can be inherent in technologies or applications. Paradoxes can also come from poor organizational or business structure. The method for innovation around paradoxes is as follows:

1. Identify paradoxes.

2. Innovate solutions around paradoxes.

3. Document and verify solutions.

Anecdote

Some years ago, we at Nokia were looking at how to create a contact list for users who did not want other people to see certain contacts. Protecting some or all contacts with a password was too cumbersome and a pain point for the target users. This paradox made us think of different and simpler solutions, and the innovation turned into a patent that was later rewarded by Nokia with an extraordinary invention prize.[1]

The solution was to allow the user to mark contact entries as hidden. These contacts would then not show up when scrolling the contacts list. However, if the user used the search function and specifically typed a certain number of characters of the hidden name, then the contact entry would show up. The paradox turned from a potential pain point into a simple but true user experience innovation.

Step 1: Identify Paradoxes

The best paradoxes for user experience innovation are paradoxes caused by conflicting user needs, conflicting core tasks, or pain points. The reason why these elements are good for user experience innovation is that they inherently contain the user needs of the target users, and hence they will give a good chance for finding user experience innovation covering a real user need.

In this chapter, I will use a piece of video-editing software as the example product. The product is intended for nontechnical people who have a need for a simple tool to create short movies based on still photos and maybe a few video clips. The process of identifying the target users, their needs, and the core tasks has revealed the paradoxes shown in Figure 15-1.

---

[1] See patent number WO2008022758

Figure 15-1. Paradoxes for video editor software

Step 2: Innovate Solutions Around Paradoxes

You are now ready for innovating around your paradoxes. You can use the previously created drawing with your paradoxes as a starting point. I will use the paradoxes from Figure 15-1 as examples to work from.

Begin by inviting colleagues and maybe some lead users to a small workshop. There you can brainstorm to find solutions for your paradoxes. The work is not easy. But bring the right group together and create the right atmosphere. You will be sometimes be surprised at the creativity that results.

Innovating around paradoxes is about seeing the paradox as a challenge. The solutions will very much depend on the type of paradox you're dealing with. Following I have given some guidance for solutions to paradoxes that are common.

Simplicity vs. Functionality

Simplicity vs. functionality (Figure 15-2) is a classical paradox that most products have. It is probably the most profound paradox in products.

Figure 15-2. Classical user experience paradox: Simplicity vs. functionality

If your paradox is that your target users want something to be very simple and at the same time they want hundreds or thousands of features, then you may need to look at methods for making your core tasks very simple but hiding advanced and less used options deeper into the system.

- For a remote control, you would want to put solutions for core tasks on dedicated keys, but hide solutions for less important tasks in onscreen menus.

- If you are designing a mobile device, you can choose to have functions related to core tasks directly accessible from a soft key or touch screen, but hide other functions in deeper menus.

- If you are designing a word processor, video-editing software, web page creation software, or similar, you might provide templates that are easy to understand but give the user a chance to use more advanced features.

- You might choose to displace more advanced functions, as described in Chapter 12. For example, if you are designing a device, you might choose to move more complex functions to another platform where these functions can be created with a good user experience (e.g., through PC software).

- You might profile specific users to find out their needs, and then hide unnecessary information and functions from them as needed.

Sometimes a good approach is simply limiting the functionality of your product to what 90 percent of your users will use. Yes, you will get complaints from some advanced users, but if the overall user experience is improved, this may be an option.

For the video-editing software used in this example, you might want to provide a simple step-by-step method for converting an entire folder of photos into a movie using different templates.

Anecdote

When I got my first iPod from Apple many years back, I often found myself wanting to change the music track information that had been labeled incorrectly (e.g., a mis-spelled artist or a wrong title). I knew that I could change the information on my PC through iTunes, but it annoyed me a little bit that I could not do it on the device.

In this case, Apple made a choice for me, which I personally—as a pretty tech-savvy user—did not appreciate. But I realized that I was not an average user. Apple decided—I guess deliberately—to displace the complexity to the PC platform.

Mismatch Between Need and Actual Usage

If your identified paradox is about functionality that the users claim to desire and need, but that they do not use, you may have a problem with the user experience for that functionality. This is a very common paradox. Maybe you have hidden a poten-tial core task too much or maybe your solution for accomplishing this core task is simply not optimal.

In other words, you have a pain point. In this case, you may want to refer to Chapter 9 and review the process for innovating around painpoints.

Relying on Other Products for Core Tasks

Another common paradox is that your entire user experience depends on other products to perform some of the core tasks of your product. This paradox is hence created by your ecosystem.

If you are designing a mobile phone, you may be dependent on network infra-structure, as well as complex user settings to allow the user to access the Internet. If you are designing video-editing software, you may depend on complex third-party software to allow the user to burn a DVD.

In these cases you want to remove or reduce the dependence on other pro-ducts. You need to find workarounds or dedicated solutions to solve this paradox. If you are designing a mobile device, you may for instance want to preload settings for every mobile phone operator in the world to ensure that the user can immediately access the Internet.

If your users are unfamiliar with specific third-party solutions that they cur-rently need to use external products for, you will probably want to integrate simple solutions for these into your products. If you, for example, design video-editing software, you may choose to integrate a simple and easy-to-use DVD-burning ap-plication into your software.

Multiple Target User Groups with Conflicting Needs

Another classical paradox comes from conflicting needs for your different target user groups. In some cases this is because you have defined your target users in the wrong way, and you may need to reduce your focus to fewer target users. In other cases, this situation is less simple.

Imagine that you have designed a mobile phone for young, low-income users in entry markets, but it ends up selling very well among elderly people in mature markets who have conflicting needs. In this case you can of course choose to remove the device from your sales channels to mature markets, but doing so will just give you less profit. A better solution may be to create variants of your product to suit the different user needs. Or you can design a new, optimized, similarly sized and priced product for the elderly in mature markets.

In some cases you may also be able to resolve conflicting needs from different target users inside the same product. You can, for example, apply different user experiences depending on the profile of the user. You can use an adaptive user interface, which will optimize the interaction for your different user needs. Or you can allow users to choose different profiles based on their specific needs and requirements.

Business Structure vs. End-User Needs

Another classical paradox involves conflicting requirements between business needs and user needs. Your business may, for example, require that the web page you are designing be plastered with banner commercials, but this may be in direct conflict with the end-user needs. Another example would be designing a smart phone where you want to expand usage of Internet and download services, but where doing so may be in initial conflict with the users' need for simplicity.

In such situations you may need to look at solutions that satisfy both sets of conflicting requirements. This can be very challenging, and there will be compromises. But if you manage to find solutions that satisfy both business needs and end users, then you may well be able to design a successful user experience innovation.

What you first want to ensure is that the user experience does not suffer too much. If you are designing a web page and your banner commercials make users leave your web page quickly, then you will lose your customers and your business. Maybe you can place banner commercials in certain areas where the user experience will not suffer too much. Maybe you can design intelligence into your web page so that banner commercials will be relevant to the user in a given situation. This will not only make users visit the page more frequently, but it may also add value for the user.

Anecdote

Google search is a good example of intelligent placement of commercials. The commercials almost always depend on the search string that the user has typed. The amount of ads is limited in the actual search results and hence doesn't reduce the overall user experience too much. In fact, the ads may even be of benefit to the user experience, if the user actually wants to click on one of the listed ad links.

If you are designing a piece of video-editing software where you want to invite users to purchase the product, you will need to first get people hooked on your product. This can be done by offering enough functionality in the shareware version, and of course by having a great overall user experience of your product. But it can also be done by giving the user small, free samples of what the purchased version can offer. Just make sure not to create pain points.

Video Conversion Software Example

In our video conversion software example, the result of generating solutions for the paradoxes may look as shown in Figure 15-3.

Figure 15-3. Result of innovation around paradoxes in the video-editing software example

Step 3: Document and Verify Solutions

As with all previously described user experience innovation methods, you again need to document and verify your solutions. For further details on verification, please refer to Chapter 18.

Summary

As mentioned, you will use user needs, core tasks, and pain points actively in the process of innovating solutions for paradoxes. But the approach you choose will depend on the nature of your paradox and your product.

In this chapter I have shown you tangible methods to solve what might seem like inherent problems in your product—paradoxes—for creating potentially successful user experience innovation.

Solving paradoxes may seem like an impossible task, but it can also be seen as a real goldmine for potential innovation. If you solve some or all of your paradoxes, your product will improve considerably and you may even reach more target user groups with your product.

Innovating Around Context Awareness

Context awareness is the ability for a device, system, or web page to know the context that the user (or the product) is in. In several ways, context awareness can be seen as a separate technology that enables the product to detect things like where the user is, what time it is, what level of experience the user has, what the user has done before, what interests the user has, what the user may do next, and even what mood the user is in. Context awareness can be achieved by using technologies like GPS, IP address identification, user action history, sensors, timing devices, questionnaires, and similar.

Even though context awareness is "just" a technology, it is also a great source of user experience innovation. By knowing your user and the situation or mood he is in, you can provide a much more optimized user experience. You can tailor the solutions for the needs of the specific user, or even to the different needs of a particular user at a given time.

You can identify the general needs of your target users before designing the product, but with context awareness you can potentially detect which needs the user has right now. You may even be able to guess the tasks he is about to accomplish and the desires he has, also right now.

Context awareness can create positive surprises and wow, since you may be able to design a product that knows what the user wants.

However, context awareness requires a fine balance. Many users do not to like to be surveyed and monitored, since this touches on human needs about feeling safe and secure. Also, many users do not like when your product makes a bad guess and suggests something wrong.

The specific steps for creating innovation around context awareness are:

1. Identify target user needs.

2. Identify current sensing capabilities.

3. Innovate context awareness.

4. Document your results and verify solutions.

The approach for innovating using context awareness is similar to the process for innovation around technologies. In this chapter I will use the example of a relatively young family father (Figure 16-1) in a mature market. The product will be a modern car that has a number of sensing capabilities built in.

Figure 16-1. Car target user example: family father

Step 1: Identify Target User Needs

As always, you need to identify the needs of the target users, as already described in previous chapters. In the case of a car targeted for family fathers in mature markets, the needs could look as shown in Figure 16-2.

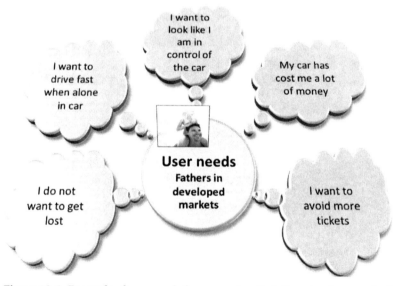

Figure 16-2. Example of user needs for young family fathers buying cars in developed markets

Step 2: Identify Current Sensing Capabilities

The next step is to list what your product is currently—or potentially—able to identify about the user, where the user is, and what the user typically does with your product. You want to list all the obvious sensor inputs that you already have (such as the location of the user, time of the day, date, other programs running at the same time, etc.), but you also want to list other elements that could potentially tell you more about the user and the context she is in right now. For example:

- If you are designing a smart phone, the phone will know the exact time, which country the device is in, and maybe even the exact location of the phone.

- If you are designing a washing machine, the machine may over time learn which programs are typically used.

- If you are designing a mobile phone or a website, your product may over time learn which functions the user is typically using, as well as when the functions are used.

- If you are designing a social website, you may detect the typical usage pattern of a specific user.

At this stage, it is OK to list only the technologies or sensors available on the device that could *potentially* detect any contextual information.

For the car example, the result could look like that in Figure 16-3. I am here assuming that the car is already equipped with a number of sensors that are already common in modern cars.

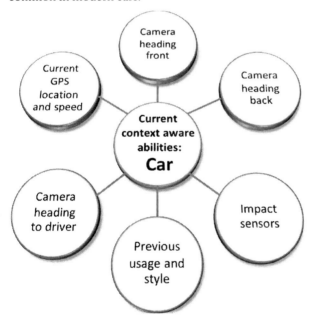

Figure 16-3. Current context awareness abilities for the car example

Step 3: Innovate Context Awareness Abilities

The next step is to innovate potential abilities from the current contextual information that you can gather about your user. You will want to combine this information with user needs, and how a user spends his or her typical day.

Context-aware user experience innovation is very much about looking at existing knowledge about user behavior and needs, and then combining it with the insights and information that you already have about the user. It is also about identifying new potential information that you can gather using the existing sensing abilities that your product already has.

Since finding current context-aware capabilities of your product is in itself an innovation task, you want at this stage to gather a small team of cross-functional colleagues and ideally some lead users for a session. What you are looking for in this innovation session is new contextual information about the user that can be deduced from your existing sensors and insights.

You will want to look at the combination of current user needs, existing knowledge of your users, and the technologies at hand in order to guess what the user may want to do. This combination will become your starting point for the user experience innovation process.

If you are, for example, designing a washing machine, you may from consumer insights (or from previous usage) know that your target users will often want to fill up and prepare the washing machine in the morning before they go to work. You may from a specific user's usage pattern know that the user typically sets the delay timer to six hours on Mondays, five hours on Fridays, and so on. And hence you already have a valuable insight about the specific user. You have in other words found context awareness information that you can use for user experience innovation.

If you are designing a smart phone, you may know that your typical users commute to work in the morning. Motion sensors or the microphone may be able to detect whether the user is sitting on a train, on a bus, or in a car. Hence, combining information that you already know about the target users with actual contextual information from sensors may give you information that a given user is now most likely on his way to work. If the user is using a built-in GPS to find his way to work, you can actually be sure of where he is going. And you can then use this information to optimize the user experience, or even come up with further user experience innovations.

If you are designing a social website, and you trace what a specific user typically does at a specific time of the day when logging in, you can over time learn about the most desired functions that this user performs at a given time of the day or week. Combining this with insights about who the user is may give you very valuable starting points for further user experience innovation.

If you are designing a low-end mobile phone, and market research shows that most target users charge their phone at night *and* use their phone as an alarm clock, you may have an insight that can help you predict when a user wants to define a new alarm (e.g., by proposing to define a new alarm when the charging plug is inserted at night time).

In the case of the car used as an example in this chapter, you can try to combine a number of existing insights about the user with the possible information that you can gather about the specific user (where he is, who he is, what time it is, etc.). A tangible method is to use the target user needs as the basis for this task. You may also want to add other potential insights that you have about your users (e.g., from day-in-the-life sessions, market feedback, etc.).

To keep this example simple, I used only the target user needs, and then I created a drawing that combines these with the sensing inputs, as shown in Figure 16-4.

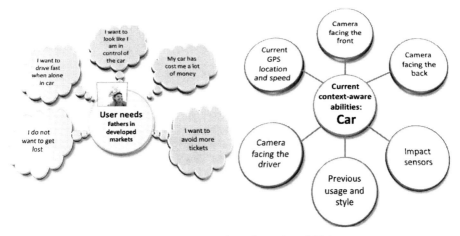

Figure 16-4. Drawing combining user needs and sensing abilities

Anecdote

One of the technologies I patented, together with my former ideation colleague Peter Dam Nielsen, automatically suggests to a user that they should set the alarm clock on their mobile device when plugging the device into a charger. Of course, the recommended alarm setting would be partly derived from the time of day and based on the previous usage pattern of the specific user (patent number WO2009077848).

Peter's and my idea is a small but intelligent example of using contextual information, where you combine consumer insights with a few simple sensors. In our case, we combined inputs from the built-in clock and the sensor detecting when a charger was plugged in, and we combined those inputs with the user's past pattern of behavior. The result is an example of using information about the user's previous patterns—both using general user insights and the current context of the user.

Now you are ready—in an innovation session—to combine what you know about the target users (family fathers in mature markets) and the sensing capabilities. You also want to be creative and, for example, invite lead users to your session. In this session you are free to combine all the knowledge about what *could* be detected about the user and his or her context. You want to combine this with known user needs and see what ideas it brings up.

In the case of the car for family fathers, you might look at ways to detect who is currently the driver. You might also want to look at ways to make the target user more confident in the car (e.g., enabling parking assistance, auto-braking when a car in front is stopping, etc.). And you might even be able to provide assistance if a car is coming very quickly from behind. Finally, you may want to use the car's cameras to detect street signs.

The results of brainstorming in such an session might look something like Figure 16-5.

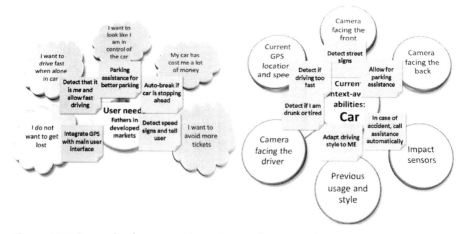

Figure 16-5. Example of user experience innovation around context awareness

As you can see from this example, using context awareness combined with knowledge about the target users can give you a number of insights and innovations.

The 2011 Ford Focus is unique because it has a large number of user experience innovations, and the car sells well based on these innovations. For example, the steering wheel vibrates when the driver changes lanes, the car can park automatically, it can identify and display current speed limits and other restrictions by using a camera facing the front, and it can brake automatically if a car is stopping ahead of you.

These user experience innovations may not be new, but they have never been of-fered in a car at this price before. And the great thing is that these innovations do not cost a fortune to implement.

As mentioned before, user experience innovations do not have to be new, but if they are relevant to the user and are applied to the right product, they may very likely be seen as true innovations.

Step 4: Document Your Results and Verify Solutions

As with any user experience innovation, you will want to document your innovations and verify them with end users. Chapter 18 talks about how to do that.

Concerns

As with many other methods described in this book, context awareness innovation has potential drawbacks. One key drawback is the risk of creating pain points. If you are guessing what the user wants in a certain situation, you will naturally be wrong in some cases. This can partially be solved by discreetly inviting the user to do things based on context awareness, rather than performing the functions automatically. If you, for example, choose to automatically change the mode of your mobile phone to silent based on contextual information, you may very easily create a serious pain point when your product makes a wrong guess. If you instead propose this option to the user, the risk is smaller, and it allows the user to stay in control.

Allowing the user to remain in control is another concern in context-aware user experience solutions. For example, you would certainly not want your car to brake in a situation where there is no real danger. Many users prefer to stay fully in control of what they do and about how much their product knows about them.

The control issue is similar to that in a personal relationship. For example, if you have a friend who frequently suggests solutions to problems for you, it may be acceptable. But if you meet a new person who tries to guess too quickly what you want or need, you will most likely reject this person, regardless of whether they're actually right.

So when designing context-aware user experience solutions, you have to be very sensitive about intimacy. For example, users may trust a close friend with the knowledge that they use a dating website, but they may not want a *product* to know this. In some cases, users may start thinking that your product is sharing their in-formation with other people, commercial websites, and so on. And then that sharing becomes a pain point; at least in the mind of the user.

Be careful with context awareness. Use the method thoughtfully. Keep privacy and control matters in mind. Do all these things right, and you can be extremely successful.

Anecdote

When I first managed to get a company car—an Audi A4—I went to the car wash after about two weeks. I drove the car into the automated car wash, switched off the engine and then checked that all windows were closed. I then opened the door, left the car, and started the car wash from the outside.

When I came back to the car, I noticed that the car window on the driver's side was half open. And when I entered the car, there was a pool of water on the floor, the car seat was soaking wet, and there was water dripping from the roof.

I ended up driving around on a cold Munich night with the heat turned up full blast and the windows open to get the steam out. I could see people looking at my car since steam came out of the windows.

Only the next day, after testing for several hours to learn how the car and window system worked, did I conclude what had happened. Audi had created a design in which the electric windows would still work after the engine was turned off, and they would also work until the driver door was closed. The reason for that design was probably to allow users to close any windows if they forgot after turning off the engine. So when I opened the door in the car wash, I must have accidentally pressed the button for opening the window (and yes, the button was "conveniently" placed next to the door handle). The car had a function to fully open the windows when the key was just pressed once, and the window must have then stopped half-way when the car detected that I closed the door again.

This story is an example of not keeping the user in control—and it is also a brilliant example of how a function designed to create positive surprises can become a serious pain point.

Summary

As you have learned, context awareness can be a great source for user experience innovation. Many products already today contain a number of sensing technologies, not least mobile phones and smart phones, and it is likely that these technologies could become available also in other device types. Using the methods described in this chapter, you may be able to create successful user experience innovations for your product.

CHAPTER

Innovating Around New Products and Users

17

The previous chapters educated you on tangible methods for identifying or defining target users, identifying user needs, and creating innovation around technologies, applications, pain points, core tasks, and a number of other elements. Without even knowing it, you may now be a user experience innovator. This applies especially if you have tried several of the previously described methods in practice already.

Becoming a successful user experience innovator is about trying things out. Reading will give you knowledge and ideas about how to solve problems, but trying things will give you skills and experience. Every time you try out the described methods, or your own variants of the methods, you will learn new things—as well as new methods. So try the methods out and discover what works for you.

Learning to Design for Great User Experience

In this chapter I will combine most of the methods you have learned so far to describe how to create successful user experience innovations for an existing product or a product targeted for new target users. With most of the previous methods, I assumed that you already had a more or less fixed product that you needed to create successful user experience innovations for. In this chapter, we will assume that the product you are designing is much more open when it comes to supported target users, technologies, applications, and—if a device—form factors, keypad layout, display size, and so forth. In practice, you will almost never be in a situation where you have the freedom to design just any new product. The most common scenario is that you need to design a product that is similar to the products that your company is already designing, but with a new group of target users. Here are some examples:

- Your company already has a social website for young users, and your task is to design a social website for mature users or people with special interests.

- Your company already has success with a TV set designed for most users, and your task is to create an optimized TV specifically for teenagers.

- Your company designs washing machines, and your new task is to design the user experience for a tumble dryer.

- Your company is a mobile device manufacturer, and your task is to design a smart phone for a new target user group (e.g., teenagers or mature users).

Figure 17-1 shows the overall steps that may be needed for creating successful user experience innovation for a product for new target users.

In most situations you will in this case need to start the user experience innovation process from the beginning. And you will certainly need to find out more about your new target users as the first step.

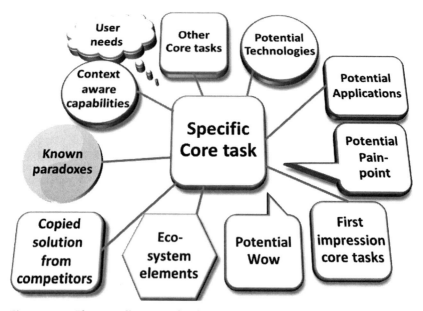

Figure 17-1. The overall approach when creating user experience innovation for core tasks for a product for new target users

Steps Needed to Design for Successful User Experience

When designing a product for new target users or a new type of product, you'll need to go through almost all the previously described methods in this book. I have changed the order of the steps to optimize the design process for a new product and a product with a new target user group. Here are the steps:

1. Identify or define your target users.
2. Identify target user needs.
3. Find and prioritize core tasks for new target users.

4. Identify key core tasks.

5. Design and innovate basic user experience elements.

6. Identify and design needed technologies.

7. Identify applications and innovate.

8. Design your product.

In this chapter I will go through all the steps listed above. However, I'll reference previous chapters to avoid repeating myself too much.

This chapter's example will look at designing the basics of a touch-enabled mobile device targeted for mature adults in developed markets. The initial product, shown in Figure 17-2, is hence intentionally left almost blank, since the assumption is that we're designing this product more or less from scratch. But two things are fixed: the target group and the touch screen technology.

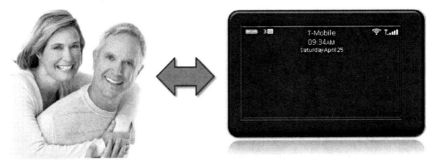

Figure 17-2. Touch-enabled mobile device for mature adults in developed markets

Let us assume that the decision for targeting mature adults with a touch-driven mobile device comes from thorough market research indicating that mature adults in developed markets have a high disposable income, and that they will also likely purchase a device with a large touch display. It is also assumed that this target group is likely to start slowly adopting this touch technology.

Step 1: Identify or Define Your Target Users

Identifying or defining a target user group is essential for any innovation around user experience. This applies when designing new products. Chapter 3 talks about how to identify a target group, so refer to that if you need a refresher.

Often, your target user group will already be defined, based on, for example, market research and market insights. But even if this is the case, you will still want to interview target users to find their needs and potential core tasks for your product. In the mobile device example, the target user group has already been identified as mature adults in developed markets.

Step 2: Identify Target User Needs

The next—and probably most essential—thing you want to do is get into the heads of your target users. Before starting any design or innovation, you need to know much more about *who* the target users are and what their needs are. In particular, you want to know what their needs are for the type of product you are designing.

Identifying user needs can be achieved through market research, interviews, or some of the other methods described in Chapter 4. In the example of a touch device for mature adults, let us assume that you have identified as the most essential user needs those shown in Figure 17-3.

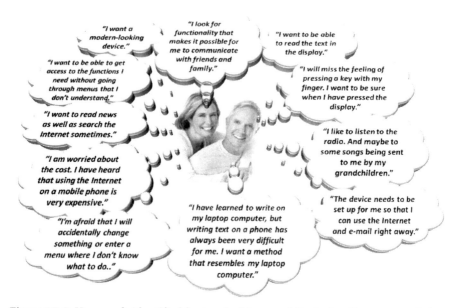

Figure 17-3. User needs identified for touch-driven mobile devices for mature adults

Step 3: Find and Prioritize Core Tasks for New Target Users

When designing a new product—or when optimizing an existing product for other target users—it is equally important to identify the core tasks of your user group. Chapter 5 talks about the importance of core tasks and gives a method for identifying them.

When I described methods for identifying core tasks in Chapter 5, I focused on getting information from your existing users (interviewing, measuring, web surveys, etc.). But how do you find the core tasks for a target user group that is not yet using your product? How do you find core tasks for a product that maybe does not even exist yet?

It is in fact not that difficult to identify core tasks for a product not yet in use or existence. You simply need to find a number of representatives from the target user group and interview them about their expectations on what they may use in your product.

When you prepare your interviews, you will use the target user needs actively. You can, for example, based on the user needs, create a list of potential core tasks in advance. Do not limit that list of tasks to assumed available technologies and applications on the device. If there is a user need for certain functionality that requires new hardware or applications, you should list tasks related to this as well. You may also want to look at potential competitor products to see which core tasks they solve and which could be relevant for your target users.

Each of the tasks you come up with should be specific enough to allow creating innovations around them later on. However, asking a user to prioritize 100 or more tasks will most likely produce an unreliable result, so you may also want to combine small core tasks into larger, more overall tasks. For example, driving a car is an overall task consisting of numerous, more granular tasks such as steering, accelerating, braking, and so forth.

▓ **Note** If you really insist on having hundreds of tasks prioritized by target users—or if your product requires this—then you can choose to split the tasks into two or more groups, and simply give different users different core tasks to prioritize. But keep in mind that very few products in this world have hundreds of potential core tasks, so try to restrict yourself based on common sense.

You can then ask the target users to categorize each of the core tasks that you have prepared; for example, you can ask the target users to rate each potential task by putting it in a different category (e.g., Very Important, Important, Less Important, Not Important, etc.). Remember to allow target users to also add their own tasks during this exercise, since you may have overlooked potentially important tasks for your product when preparing for the interview.

Figure 17-4 shows how this exercise might turn out with the target users in the touch mobile device example. (The list hasn't been verified with actual mature target users; it serves purely as an example in this book.)

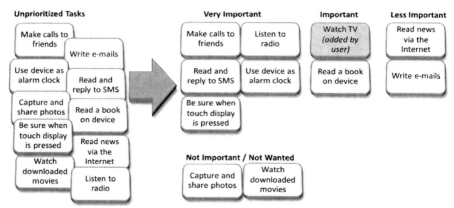

Figure 17-4. Example of prioritizing core tasks in the mobile device example

Sometimes when you find your core tasks, you may realize that the product you are designing may be over the top for the tasks at hand. This may lead you to radically reconsider whether you are designing the right type of product. Is it, for example, worth designing a relatively expensive touch-enabled mobile device if the core tasks for the target users are basic call handling, alarm clock functionality, and replying to messages?

However, it may not be as simple as creating what you feel is the right type of product. The target users may actually desire an over-the-top product anyway, even though their core tasks are limited. In the case of the touch display, the target users may desire such a product based on general market trends, and you should thus try to create a superb user experience for the core tasks within the given product scope.

Step 4: Identify Key Core Tasks

In the initial design of your product, you will primarily focus on your top core tasks. This will ensure that the product you design is really targeted to your customers and not compromised by lower-priority tasks.

Depending on the product, you might have between one and ten top core tasks. Having more tasks may mean that you'll lose focus or that you have defined your target user group to be too broad.

For the touch-enabled mobile device for mature adults, the top core task list could as an example look like that shown in Figure 17-5.

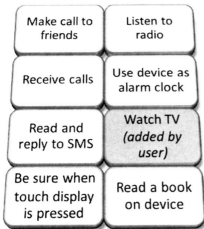

Figure 17-5. Example of top eight core tasks identified for the touch-enabled device for mature adults

Step 5: Design and Innovate Basic User Experience Elements

The next step is to design the basic user experience of your product. Chapter 6 covers how to do this with respect to innovating around core tasks.

If you are designing a web page, you want to innovate guidelines for the visual style of your product, as well as the basic user experience elements for the page (menu style, whether to include drop-down lists, security, etc.). You also want at this stage to create a basic layout or wireframe of your web page. This is done by using the top core tasks, as well as general insights involving the needs of the target users.

If you are designing a device, you also want to design the basic physical input and output elements, such as the keypad, touch interaction principles, display, LEDs, vibration feedback, and so on.

There may be several solutions for solving each of the tasks, and you may need to prototype a number of different solutions and verify them with users until you have found a suitable solution. The process is similar to that described in Chapter 6, except that this time you do not have any existing solutions for your core tasks yet.

You will need to take each top core task one by one, and work through it in a workshop within a cross-functional team, and potentially with lead users. Focus in each workshop on creating an innovative user experience to solve the core task at hand. During these user experience innovation sessions, you can use competitor products as inspiration, you can use copying, you can focus on wows and positive surprises, and you can look at the ecosystem and the first impression.

Figure 17-6 shows how the result of an innovation session for a single top core task could look for the touch-enabled mobile device.

Figure 17-6. Example of user experience innovation around a single key core task

For each core task, you should easily find a number of solutions, and you should do some initial prototyping of each of these solutions. Create working proto-types, paper prototypes, Flash animations, videos, mechanical mock-ups or what-ever else works for you.

The format of your prototype depends on the nature of your product, your solu-tion, and the target users. Generally, there is no reason to overdo prototypes at this stage of product creation. However, it is important that the target users fully under-stand and relate to your solution when they see your prototype during the verification later. The main goal is to ideally create multiple prototypes of solutions for each of the key core tasks, which can then be evaluated with target users.

▓ **Note** Prototyping and verification is described further in Chapter 18.

I want to emphasise that in this step it is important to focus very much on target user needs and key core tasks. A common mistake is to more or less reuse an exist-ing product and then simply add a few functions for the new target user group. Doing so will very seldom give successful user experience innovations. Another mis-take is to try to use too many core tasks when designing the product. The key goal of this part of the process is to create a product optimized for the target users and their top core tasks.

Verification of the concepts with target users is essential at this stage, since you can save a lot of time if you can filter out wrong ideas. You can use multiple solutions and prototypes for each core task, thereby giving users the possibility of choosing from multiple solutions. In some cases, you may find that several of your solutions are suitable and could provide successful user experience innovations. In such cases, you may need to prioritize based on, for example, cost and capability, if you do not want to offer *all* solutions.

It may in some cases be an advantage to have multiple solutions for the same core task to satisfy different user needs and different usage situations. However, creating too many different solutions for the same core task may easily result in creating pain points or a product that has too many options for performing the same task. So this specific situation is a balancing act.

In some cases when verifying your solutions with target users, you may find that none of your solutions are really optimal, even if some of your solutions may have some good elements. This is where an iterative approach is essential. You will basically go back and redo your innovation sessions again, of course using the findings from your first verification rounds. How many iterations you need depends on the nature of your product, on the quality of your previous innovation sessions, and on how well you have identified your target user needs and core tasks.

In the example of the mobile device for mature users, I will assume that a number of iterations of innovation sessions, prototyping, and user verifications have led to the basic interaction elements for the mobile device shown in Figure 17-7.

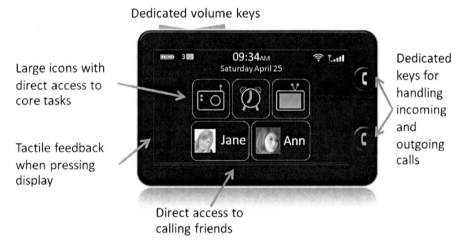

Figure 17-7. Example of basic interaction elements identified for the touch mobile device

Step 6: Identify and Design Needed Technologies

After you have a basic user experience structure in place, you are ready to innovate the user experience around the technologies that you have already planned for your product and those that you may need to add to satisfy the target user needs. Use the approach in Chapter 7 for innovating around technologies that you already plan to use. Begin with the core tasks to help in identifying new potential technologies that you may need to add to your web page, system, or device.

If you are designing a web page for new target users, and you have identified that these users have a core task that involves protecting their data, you should consider focusing on easy-to-use and innovative password and login technologies. If your users have a core task of finding products easily on your web page, you should consider investing in or developing good product search algorithms that fit those target users.

If you are designing a touch-enabled mobile device for mature users and these users have core tasks such as listening to the radio and watching TV, then you should seriously consider adding radio and TV receiver technology to your device. Whether you choose to support TV using technologies like DVB-H or DVB-T, or whether you simply design great user experience solutions for Internet streaming of TV will depend on your ecosystem, the market requirements, and the regional target user needs. Figure 17-8 shows how an icon to support TV might look on our mobile device.

Figure 17-8. Technology for TV added for the mobile device example

If the users of your touch-enabled mobile device have a profound need to get tactile feedback when using your touch device, you can consider adding dedicated dome-based keys. Or you can add tactility (virtual or physical) to your touch device. Figure 17-9 shows one possible method of adding feedback to a touch panel.

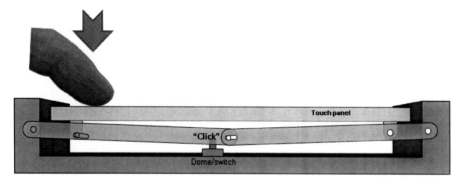

Figure 17-9. Touch pad with mechanical movement and click functionality

You will certainly want to verify the technologies with target users. You should also innovate around each technology as described in Chapter 7.

Anecdote

Tactility for touch-operated smart phones may be a true need for a number of users (e.g., mature users or users using the device while, for example, walking). Some existing solutions for achieving tactility include vibrating feedback.

During my time at Nokia, we invented a mechanism for which the touch area is depressed when touched, similar to a normal dome-based key. Providing a touch area that actually moves downward when pressed not only offers brilliant tactility, but lends a new dimension to touch pads. It allows the user to distinguish between touching the display gently and actually pressing the display, which can allow for a number of potentially successful user experience innovations.

Gently touching the display could e.g. zoom the area you are about to select, and depressing the display could actually select the item[1] This concept was later used in a slightly different implementation by RIM in its SurePress Touch Screen technology applied to its BlackBerry Storm device.

Step 7: Identify Applications and Innovate

The next step is to identify the applications of your product. This time you may want to look not only at the top core tasks for your target users, but also at lower-priority core tasks. You will hence—based on the target user needs and core tasks—create a list of the applications that your product should contain.

Even though the core tasks are the focus in this step, it is vital also keep the target users and their user needs in mind. If "making calls to friends" is identified as a core task, then many designers might automatically say, "We can use the call-handling and contact list functionality from our previous product designed for business users." This may not, however, be suitable for the needs of the new group of target users.

If you are designing an electronic car key, you might limit your applications to opening doors, closing doors, and starting the engine. If you also identify the lower-priority core task of opening the trunk, you might consider adding that as an application as well.

For more complex products, the list of applications might be longer, but you should try to avoid the common mistake of simply filling your product with all applications that any potential user might like to use. So, it is important to follow the core tasks identified for the target users. However, there may be regulations or standards that need to be followed, which may require adding further applications.

---

[1] Patent number US 2009051661, WO2009050622 etc

When the applications have been identified, it is essential to verify the list of with target users. You should also use the previously described method from Chapter 8 to create successful user experiences around applications.

Going through all the steps and applications needed for the touch-enabled mobile device would be too much to do in this book, but Figure 17-10 shows how an extract of the results might look.

Application list:
- Simplified contacts list with photos
  - TV player
  - Radio player
  - Alarm clock
  - Book reader
- Simplified text sending and receiving

Figure 17-10. Shortened application list for the touch-enabled mobile device for mature users

Step 8: Design Your Product

When you have the list of applications for your product, you are ready to start designing your product. It will be too extensive to describe all the needed steps here, but you will certainly use many if not all of the methods described earlier in this book. You should, for example, look at the first impression of your product, innovate around the ecosystem, and create wows and positive surprises. You should also try to foresee pain points and create successful user experiences around these.

The key message for this part of the process is to always keep the target users, their needs, and their core tasks in mind. It is easy during this part of the process to get carried away and design applications and elements that you would like yourself, rather than things that the target users want.

Another important thing to emphasize for the design process is involving target users as much as you can. Involving users does not have to mean performing extensive, cumbersome, and expensive usability tests; it can simply mean calling target users that you already have been in contact with, and maybe dropping them an e-mail or visiting them to present new ideas.

Involving users at a very early stage may save you a lot of time later, since you can avoid creating finalized designs of functionality that the users may not want at all. It will also ensure that the user experience of your product is optimal.

Summary

This chapter has shown you how to use the processes described in previous chapters to actually create a new product for new target users. During this process, it's important to keep focus on the target user needs and core tasks. Also, by keeping the target users in the loop throughout the process, you will have a good chance of creating a successful user experience for your product.

Prototyping and Verifying Solutions

In the previous chapters I emphasized the need for verifying user experience innovations, and I emphasized the need to verify your core tasks, your pain points, and your wows.

One common mistake with verification is almost finishing your design and only then verifying your solutions. In this book I have mentioned a number of methods to verify not only solutions, but also raw ideas, core tasks, causes of pain points, and so forth. It is of utmost importance that you verify at every step during your innovation process. And you will *have* to do this with your target users. No one else can verify for you, and if you end up on the wrong track for a solution, you may waste valuable time and resources.

The good thing is that verification is not difficult at all. The trick with verification is to verify your results from the innovation process at all stages. Verification may be less accurate at an early stage of the innovation, but it is always better to do some verification up front and get a fuzzy picture that you can refine later than to do no verification at all and head in a completely wrong direction.

For example, if you come up with a wrong cause for a serious pain point and you do not verify the cause, you may go a very long way down the innovation path before realizing this mistake. And you will not only have used a lot of time and resources designing a solution for something that the end user may not need, but you will also have missed the opportunity to solve the real cause of your pain point.

You can find a huge amount of literature and a number of articles about different methods for verifying your results and innovations, so in this chapter I will go through only the methods that I know are very effective. Depending on what you are verifying, the steps may vary slightly, but you will usually need to follow the steps described in the following sections.

Prototyping

Prototyping may sound like creating fully functional implementations of your ideas and thoughts, but in this sense it covers any method that visualizes or describes an idea.

Here are some examples:

- If you want to verify a pain point, you might as the prototype simply take a photo of a person experiencing the pain point and discuss this photo with the user. You might also have the user experience the pain point on your existing product and witness their reactions, hereby simply using your existing product as a prototype.

- If you want to verify core tasks, you might as prototype use multiple photos or illustrations in a cartoon-like manner. Or you might create a small video using your colleagues as actors.

- If you want to verify solutions, you might create simulations or simple paper prototypes.

If you feel that prototyping a specific solution is complex, then it is most likely because your solution is too complex, and you may want to look at the user experience of your solution again.

In the following sections, I will go through some easy and effective ways to create prototypes.

Photos and Illustrations

If you want to verify a certain core task or pain point, using simple photos is a very easy and effective method. In some situations you may have the need to manipulate the photo to emphasize the situation.

If you want to create a prototype of a device or a screenshot, you can use handmade sketches, simple drawing tools, or a presentation program. Figure 18-1 shows some of the prototypes that I created for this book (the total creation time was around one hour). I cannot sketch or use Photoshop well, so my preferred tool is Microsoft PowerPoint. Are these prototypes perfect? No, and they should *not* be, since trying to make them perfect will waste time at an early stage of the innovation process. What is important is that the prototype tells the story that you are trying to tell the users. And that is a key element when, for example, approaching users with your early user experience innovation ideas. My proposal is that you use the tools that you feel comfortable with and that allow you to create prototypes quickly. If you are good at making sketches by hand or with graphics tools, then use these methods. If you can create great prototypes with clay or LEGO bricks, feel free. The trick is not to be fixed to a single tool or set of tools. Limiting yourself will often just deter you from what you really want to achieve: telling the user about your concept, a pain point, or a feature.

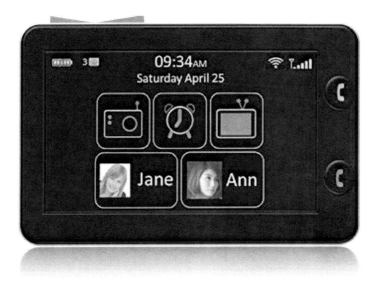

Figure 18-1. Two prototypes used in this book

Cartoons and Storyboards

If you want to verify core tasks, solutions, positive surprises, or pain points, you might use small storyboards with situations that you either draw yourself or assemble using photos. These stories can be used to describe specific situations and problems, as well as potential solutions.

Flash Videos and Simulations

If you want to verify solutions that have several interaction elements or are very visual, you may want to create a short Flash video or an interactive Flash simulation. Some people can create extremely powerful Flash videos and interactive simulations in almost no time. This approach can be very useful for verifying basic concepts for your web page, device, or similar.

Videos

Creating videos using your colleagues as actors (Figure 18-2) can be a quick and easy way to create prototypes explaining pain points, core tasks, user needs, or even solutions and ideas.

Figure 18-2. Video prototyping

Paper Prototypes

Simple paper prototypes can be very effective for testing interaction flows. Paper prototypes can be very simple hand drawings, screenshots, or illustrations that you have created.

Verification

When you have created your prototype, you will need to verify it with target users. When you want to learn about target users—for example, to learn about their core tasks or pain points—you will of course need to approach them in some way. There already exists extensive literature on how to verify innovations and achieve insights from target users, but in the following sections I will briefly introduce some methods that I have myself used with success.

User Interviews

Much verification can be done by interviewing target users. You can do this on the street, in their homes via e-mail, or by phone. Face-to-face meetings in the user's natural environment usually give the best results.

If you are trying to find or verify user needs, you may use professional interviewers for your task, but with some practice you may quickly learn to do it yourself. To verify core tasks, pain points, and so on, you want to present the users with concrete examples of the tasks or pain points using prototypes.

Market Research

Market research is good for finding and verifying target users and end-user needs. Verifying core tasks and solutions may also be possible using market research, but usually interviews or usability tests are better for these.

Usability Tests

Usability tests are useful for verifying solutions and ideas that are pretty mature and for which you can present the user with paper prototypes, simulations, or similar. Usability tests may be very relevant if testing an application or technology that is almost finalized.

When performing usability tests, you will mostly focus on the new application or element that you've designed, but you can also use additional findings that the usability tests may reveal (e.g., for identifying potential future needs, overlooked core tasks, or pain points).

Lead User Workshops

Lead user workshops are ideal not only for revealing user needs, core tasks, and pain points, but also for actually innovating new user experience elements. Chapter 13 of this book goes into detail on this type of workshop.

Summary

In this short chapter I have given you some ideas on how to prototype your solutions and ideas. I have also described how you can verify solutions without using huge amounts of resources. Remember to prototype and verify at different—or ideally all—stages along the way in your product development process. Don't wait until the very end, when you have a fully designed product, only to find out that you've gone a long way down the wrong path.

Meeting Organizational Challenges

User experience specialists and innovators seem to face the same problems no matter what type of organization they're in. In small companies, you will need to face the owner(s), who will often tell you that user experience innovation is a waste of time, and the company should rather focus on bringing new technologies or products to the market. In large corporations, you may feel squeezed between software and other engineers who say that it will take a very long time to implement your innovation, and that they are busy creating new technologies required for the next range of products.

In my (nonstatistical) mind, I guess that in more than 90 percent of companies and organizations in this world, user experience experts, innovators, and designers often feel overlooked and underappreciated. This is why I chose to include this chapter, which hopefully will give you, as a person with a focus on user experiences, some ammunition and methods to use in your specific company or organization.

In my belief, user experience innovation will become the battleground in almost *all* consumer businesses within a few years. So why are companies and organizations so reluctant to embrace this new winning approach?

For one, reluctance to change and stubbornness (Figure 19-1) inside your organization may be a key factor (even if this stubbornness may leave your company obsolete).

Figure 19-1. Stubbornness is often a key reason for not focusing on user experience innovation.

In the following sections, I will go through some of the typical problems that you may face in organizations of all sizes when trying to pitch your user experience innovations. And I will propose some methods that may—or may not—work in your situation and organization.

Technology vs. User Experience

One typical problem is that technology is seen as more important than the user experience. Maybe you are working at a company where you are the only one who cares about the user experience, or where the group of people focusing on user experience is often overlooked. Other times you as user experience designer may be reduced to perform usability tests of the final product. You may personally be trying hard to make the rest of the organization see how important a good user experience is. But in many businesses, user experience still is not valued or seen as a competitive element.

I still see devices—for example, in the medical industry that require weeks of training, but why waste a doctor's time on training if the problem could be solved with an improved user experience? I still see cars that have absolutely unintuitive interaction panels. When did all car drivers have to become engineers to operate their vehicles?

There are many reasons why devices, software, and systems in certain industries are designed to be difficult to use. But most of the time there's no need for this to be the case. For instance, in the medical business you may need to comply with very strict standards, but these standards very rarely relate to the user experience. And I have never in my life seen any standard saying that a certain product *has* to be difficult to use. Not even if the product is operated by a surgeon during a surgery. And would you want a surgeon to have to look in a manual many times during a surgery (Figure 19-2) to check how to operate a specific device? I have never seen a standard saying that a certain product should require two or more weeks of training before it can be used.

Figure 19-2. Sorry, I need to look at the manual to see how to use this device.

The problem is often resistance in certain parts of the organization and with the management. The argument is often, "Our competitors make even more complex products." And maybe your company is even earning more money on training people how to use the device than on the device itself.

Resistance to creating good user experience is certainly a challenge for you as a user experience expert and/or innovator. But there are solutions, as described in previous chapters of this book.

The "I Know What the Users Want" Attitude

It is amazing how many people in your organization actually think that they know exactly what people want, and how a product should be designed. I am in no way saying that a user experience expert always knows best how to create a great product; I am just saying that when it comes to the user experience, you will be confronted with a very large number of people who will tell you that they know better.

I usually compare user experience with bringing up a child. Many people have tried bringing up a child once or twice, and hence they feel like experts in child psychology. These people will argue with experts in the area because they feel that they have the same expertise as, say, a teacher, educator, child psychologist, and so forth.

Sales managers typically know a lot about how customers react to a certain product, but do they really know what the users want? They typically know all about what the customers do *not* want, and also what the users tell them they want. This is very valuable information, but it does not necessarily tell anything about latent needs and what consumers may in reality be looking for.

Salespeople are also rarely innovative. They tend to stick to a solution that a single (important) customer has asked for. They are rarely able to see what a majority of users would want—and being creative is not part of their job description. Of course there are exceptions, and I have seen quite a few. This is not an attempt to blame salespeople (or CEOs for that matter), but rather to say that priorities are often different in different parts of your company.

Likewise, product managers often tend to solely look at what is easily marketable. This is very important, indeed, but product managers may not see underlying needs that can actually create a truly great and cool product. My impression of product managers is that they are really good at focusing on a single function or feature for a product, because they can already see how this feature can be used in marketing campaigns. But product managers often lack the capacity to see the potential if you instead create 20 small user experience improvements to the product. In my experience, 20 small improvements to the user experience of a product may sometimes have a much bigger effect in the market than a single new feature. And these improvements can even be marketed if done right. And it may be your task to explain and rectify this to the product manager.

Engineers and engineering managers typically know what is easy to implement, and hence their minds will often be skewed toward solutions that are easy to implement. This can be challenging to tackle, and you will sometimes need to understand the challenges that they have in finding solutions that are easier to implement but that still give the same user experience.

Ignorance

Ignorance and lack of knowledge are other typical reasons why you may have big challenges getting through with your user experience knowledge and innovations. I have previously argued that user experience will become the main battleground for all future innovation, but this is not commonly accepted in most companies and organizations.

Especially in smaller organizations, you will often feel alone in your views. Do not become desperate, though. It is *not* easy to change an organization that is not used to getting inputs from a person who claims to know more about what the customers want; I have basically lived my professional life in this state for 18 years.

Getting Lost in Big Organizations

I have personally experienced being lost in large organizations and organizational structures. The CEO and everyone in upper management typically want to get products on the market as quickly as possible. CEOs will typically be business educated, so they may think that *any* product will do. You, on the other hand, know that the product will not be successful in the market if certain user experience innovations are not implemented. And you personally know that without these elements, the company may end up with a product that users and analysts will see as being mediocre.

Solutions and Methods

As mentioned, I have been a user experience innovator in both small and large companies. And in both situations, it can be very challenging to make your voice heard. At the upper levels in many companies, it is all about numbers, quotas, and deadlines. In other parts of the company, it may be about satisfying a single customer. But in my humble mind, this is all a mistake. If you want to improve your numbers, then you need to improve your products. And in current markets (especially for consumer-oriented products), user experience is slowly but surely becoming a key differentiator. In other words, if you do not focus on user experience, the numbers and deadlines may no longer be relevant at all.

Following I will go through some solutions to the above challenges faced by user experience innovators. But keep in mind that they are *not* bulletproof. However, I hope that you at least get some inspiration about what you can do. Every organization and company is different, and some methods may work in one company but not others. However, I have compiled the methods that I personally feel have worked best.

Use Customer Insights

You will find yourself in a number of situations with numerous people who say that they know more about what the customers want than you do. You may be submissive, which will get you nowhere. Alternatively, you should use your insights about what the users and customers actually want.

There may be other parts of your organization that know about the customers—for example, people involved with market research functions. In this case, you will want to try to team up with your market research people.

Arguing from a customer insights point of view is a very strong method to get your ideas and opinions through. There are very few organizations and companies in this world that will officially say that they do not listen to the consumers. So what you will often experience is that people will listen when you can reliably say that 80 percent of the users have problems using this or that function in your product, or when you say that 50 percent of users have a need to do this or that with your product, and so on. So you will certainly need numbers to make your point. But you may not necessarily need extensive statistical data. If you can verify that, for example, three out of five users had serious problems using a specific part of your product, that may be enough to make your point. This will depend on the stubbornness of your organization. So use your insights, and use your data. This may even convince the most stubborn people in your organization.

Invite People to Workshops

Inviting people in your organization to user experience innovation workshops may be a very effective way to basically teach people in the organization how to keep the customers in focus. You may also want to invite lead users to some of the workshops, thereby combining direct user feedback with the methods and approaches for creating user experience innovations.

Workshops also have the wonderful advantage that almost all people attending them will see the ideas that came up as their own, and hence give more traction inside the organization to actually implement the ideas in your product. Workshops often also offer a very successful method to train people in thinking like a user experience expert or innovator.

It is important when organizing user experience innovation workshops to make them different from the normal meetings that the people in your company have (see Figure 19-3). I have personally seen many meetings in large corporations where people read and write e-mails all the way through the meeting, unless their favorite topic comes up.

You want to make your user experience workshops very different. Have the workshop in a park, inside a customer's house, or in some other interesting location. Invite real users to the workshop to loosen up the people joining the workshop. It is amazing how one comment from a single real customer can change the mind of even the most stubborn people in your organization. They can reject your point of view, but they will (hopefully) never reject the opinion of a user.

Try to approach the scope of the workshop in a unique and interesting way. For example, I have seen user experience innovation workshops held as Bingo sessions, where the participants needed to come up with enough ideas or core tasks to fill a card, I have seen workshops where the main scope was to build prototypes with LEGO bricks, and I have seen meetings held in unusual settings, such as a museum.

Figure 19-3. *Find alternative ways to hold your user experience workshops.*

In other words, try to stand out, not only to make your workshop participants get away from their daily routines, but also to make them think differently. It is OK to stand out, because as a user experience innovator you are already seen as different.

Create Cross-Functional Teams

If you are so lucky that you are able to create a cross-functional user experience team, then you have a very good chance of breaking the barriers in your organization. Cross-functional teams can create truly innovative user experience solutions that are detached from normal company thinking. Maybe your team will find mechanical or electrical solutions to a software problem. Or maybe your team of algorithm experts will find a genuine solution to create a truly new user experience. Or maybe your market research team has identified a unique user need that no one else in the market is currently covering.

Being cross-functional or multidisciplinary may vary depending on the nature of your product and organization—for example, at a web-design company, looking at mechanical solutions may not be relevant. But then you can bring in people from different levels of software development, from marketing, and even from management.

If you are not lucky enough to be able to create an isolated user experience innovation team with multiple disciplines, there is still hope. You can basically create the cross-functional team on a per-need basis, and you can invite these people for specific workshops. Most companies today allow each employee to take part in meetings and workshops that do not relate directly to their expert area. And you will actually find that these people will often love to join such workshops.

Isolated and dedicated user experience innovation teams may become a potential problem, however, since they can be seen by the rest of the organization as an unapproachable ivory tower. This can be avoided by assuring that the team members are involved also with ongoing product development, by frequent rotation of people into the team etc.

In sum, if you are the only user experience expert and innovator at a small company, you should invite people from other disciplines to your workshops. This will not only give you valuable insights, but it will also slowly direct your company and the organization to be more focused on user needs and the potential innovations hidden there.

Provide Examples from Competition

Another approach to convincing your organization about the need to focus on user experience innovation is by providing good examples. You may want to use examples from your direct competitors—for example, in cases where they have successfully gained market share due to better user experience (similar to how I've used the example of the Apple iPhone several times in this book to describe how successful user experience innovation can be created). Your product and business may be different, so find your own good examples among your competition.

So, use your competitors, and for that matter other businesses, to make your point, and to convince the people in your organization that changes are needed.

Do Internal Marketing

Internal marketing of user experience innovations cannot be emphasized enough, whether you're working at a very large organization or a small company. To be successful in internal marketing of what user experience innovation can do for your product or business area, you will again need data from real users. This data may tell you that your current product is extremely difficult to use, or it may show that your customers prefer another product. All this data will be useful.

You may also want to set up meetings with upper management to tell about why it is important to focus on the user experience, where you basically teach them about user experience and user experience innovation. In this case, you will want to have concrete data about why your company may be losing ground to competitors, and how the (lack of) user experience innovation is contributing to this. If you can even dig up some financial data about what value it would have if you focused more on user experience, so much the better. But putting a figure on the value of user experience is generally difficult.

Deliver Great Ideas and Prototypes

Bringing truly valuable ideas into your company or organization is probably one of the most effective methods of changing the attitudes about user experience innovation in your company.

Again, I would use user data to approach this challenge, and, for example, use some of the many methods already described in this book. Give management the true story about how the users see your current product. Tell the story about what your users *really* want, based on facts, insights, user tests, and so on.

You will also want to show your user experience innovation ideas with proto-types, be it with animated PowerPoint slides, Flash animations, prototypes, or similar.

Let Decision-Makers Participate in Usability Tests

Another approach to convincing people in your organization about the value of user experience is to invite people to usability tests. A usability test is a great way to convince people in organizations where user experience is not yet valued at all. Seeing real users struggle with your current product is a good eye-opener for people who believe that they know how the products are seen by users.

Conduct Street Interviews

I have already mentioned street interviews as a method for getting quick insights into the user needs and desires. Street interviews (Figure 19-4) are also good for changing the attitude in an organization toward user experience. Letting people from your organization stand face to face with your customers can be eye-opening for almost everyone within your organization.

Figure 19-4. *Street interview example*

Street interviews may apply to certain types of products, especially consumer products, but they may be trickier for technical products for which you may not likely meet your customers on the street. In this case, you may want to invite people in your organization to people's homes, to their workplaces, and so on. If you are, for example, designing products used during surgery, then invite people to a real surgery.

Involve Yourself in Specific Products

I have myself very successfully used this method. One of the best ways to show what you can contribute to for a specific product is to actually contribute to that product. The project manager who ensures on-time delivery of your product may not be your first point of contact, because they may see you as a person who suggests innovations that may take time and resources to implement. You might instead go to a product manager or some other person with a customer or user focus. This could be a product manager or a software chief with a sincere belief in creating a great product. This will depend on your organization and company, of course.

What you want to do in this case is propose tangible and highly marketable solutions, based of course on the methods described in this book.

You may need to compromise many times during this process, but your main goal is to get more and more people accepting and respecting what you can bring to the product. And the method is—as described a bit earlier—to suggest tangible solutions that may make the specificproduct great.

Teach Internally

Internal teaching is seldom a success, unless, as described previously, you use very good examples from your consumer insights, from pain points you've identified, and from competition. In my experience, the people who would voluntarily go to a teaching session on user experience and user experience innovation are few—or they may already be part of the niche group of people inside your company who have already seen the light. So, my suggestion in most cases is to rather try to sell your teaching as something else. You may use phrases such as *how to tackle our strong competition* or *bringing the company back onto the profit track*. Yes, this sounds like marketing-speak, and admittedly, it is. But successful user experience innovation may be extremely important for your company in the very near future, so why not sell it like that? There's no need to be too academic and use dull phrasings such as *user experiences are important for future products.*

In my mind, too many user experience experts and innovators make the classic mistake of being academic and claiming that user experience is complex. I disagree with this. User experience innovation is *not* academic, and it is certainly not something that only a few select companies in the world cancan do.

Summary

In this chapter, I have explained some of the many challenges that you will meet inside your company or organization when you propose your great and maybe successful user experience innovations. There is no easy way to do this, and I have personally worked for many years to make the need for user experience innovation heard in the companies that I have worked for.

We did, however, eventually manage to bring together one of the first multidisciplinary teams at Nokia, where my innovation capabilities managed to flourish. Before that I worked directly with product managers, engineers, and even CEOs for several years to push my messages through—often with success, but also many times without. I have managed to put my user experience fingerprints on a large number of specific products, and often on a case-to-case basis, simply by delivering good user experience innovation and design, with good backup from user insights and user data.

I have been behind a large number of user experience innovations launched in products, and I have seen innovations become successful when there was a true user need. I've also seen some of my innovations quickly become forgotten. But what has always driven my passion is a desire to meet a single customer who tells me how great a function that I designed works—and a desire to see millions of users using a function that I designed. And it is exactly this passion that is the most important element for facing organizational challenges, stubbornness, and so forth.

In other words, I'm not saying that this part is easy, and I'm not saying that there's one single solution, but I do think that great ideas and the right approaches to user experience will flourish in almost any organization. But it requires some work and selling.

Conclusion

I hope that you have found inspiration in many of the methods I have described in this book. User experience innovation will become the battleground in almost *all* consumer businesses within a few years. It has happened widely already within the web page design area, it has happened within the mobile phone area, and it will also happen in industries such as those involving washing machines, stereo and other music systems, remote controls, cars, and so forth. Customers will start to expect and demand reasonable user experiences for any product they purchase.

User experience innovation (especially for consumer-focused products) is nothing less than essential for survival! No company, be it a car manufacturer, a washing machine manufacturer, a social website company, or a mobile device manufacturer, will survive without focusing on user experience.

Consider Nokia. Nokia led the mobile industry for more than a decade—mainly due to a consistent flow of user experience improvements and innovations. Yet in only a few years' time, Nokia's position in the market dropped significantly, especially in the profitable smart phone sector, which is now controlled largely by Apple and Android-based products. Why the sudden drop in fortune? It was largely due to the lack of good user experience in Nokia's product line.

You will see the same trend repeat in other markets very soon. The world is changing. Customers, users, and people will demand and expect superior user experiences, and they will choose the products they purchase based on this. The change will come first in consumer-oriented products, but it will extend to professional-use products as well. If your company or organization is not currently looking into user experience innovations, you may already be too late. Focus on user experience innovation *now*.

User experience innovation is essential. Apple and Google have shown how to attack companies that were ruling the industry. They have won simply by applying relevant, novel, visible, and marketable user experience solutions and innovations to the market.

I will not claim that the methods described in this book are perfect, since perfect methods do not exist. But I can say that these methods have helped me personally to create more than 100 filed patents. They have helped me to create a number of truly successful user experience innovations for Nokia when Nokia was still seen as one of the top ten most innovative companies in the world. Begin trying out the methods, and over time you may adapt the methods for your specific product, or you may come up with your own additional methods or variants.

As an ending remark, I would like to emphasize three things that can help you create successful user experience innovation.

First is to involve the users. Find ways to involve users without spending a lot of time and money, and use existing insights and methods already available in your company. And find a way to involve your target users at every step of the iterative process—from getting input to verifying your solutions at all steps of the iterative innovation process.

The second thing is to focus on making your target users happy, or even make them fall in love with your product. Fixing small pain points in applications that are never used is a waste of time, so focus your efforts on making your core tasks and first impressions great. If you achieve those things, you will likely end up with a successful user experience.

The third thing that I want to emphasize is to make it *fun* to use your product, or at least to make it pain free. There are so many products in the world with a very poor user experience, spanning from TV remote controls to software packages to web pages. Create products that are fun to use. Success lies down that path.

—Christian Kraft, 2012

I

Index

A

Apple, 4, 14, 18

applications, 43, 75–79
  documenting results and
    processing output, 78
  identifying target user
    needs, 76
  innovating solutions, 78
  to interact with, 76
  placing in center of
    diagram, 77
  of products, 175–176

autostore function, 141

B

Bang & Olufsen, 115–116

brainstorming, 67, 162

business needs, vs. user needs,
  154–155

C

calendar example, 79

car targeted user, 158

cartoons, and storyboards, 181

Cetelco/Hagenuk, 137–138

competitors
  categorizing solutions of, 140
  examples from, as solution to
    organizational
    challenges, 191
  identifying potential solutions
    from products of, 138–139

consumer experience, user
  experience vs., 5

context awareness, 157–164
  concerns regarding, 163
  documenting results and
    verifying solutions, 163
  identifying current sensing
    capabilities, 159
  identifying target user
    needs, 158
  innovating abilities, 160–162
  intelligence and, 117–118

copying, 137–148
  concerns regarding, 147
  identifying potential solutions
    from competitor
    product, 138–139
  solutions
    categorizing competitor, 140
    innovating, 140–147
    verifying, 147

CPSIA information can be obtained at www.ICGtesting.com
Printed in the USA
LVOW110141030212

266865LV00002B/2/P